Anthony Hammond is a very experienced educator with nonformal activity related learning. Starting out as a quality control engineer, he became a teacher of mathematics at the age of 30. After working in secondary schools, community college, high schools, and a grammar school, he became an adviser and leader of alternative education for learners who do not cope with mainstream schools. He set up his own business, advising several local authorities on their alternative arrangements to educate learners out of a traditional school setting.

Anthony Hammond

Nonformal Activity Related Learning

Austin Macauley Publishers®
London * Cambridge * New York * Sharjah

A CIP catalogue record for this title is available from the British Library.

ISBN 9781035801947 (Paperback)
ISBN 9781035801954 (ePub e-book)

www.austinmacauley.com

First Published 2026
Austin Macauley Publishers Ltd®
1 Canada Square
Canary Wharf
London
E14 5AA

Dedication

My wife, Roma, who has supported, assisted and believed in my work
from the very beginning.

Acknowledgements

Jonathan Hammond, Steve Taylor, Alan Wain, Linda Bennett, John Bateman, John Huskins,
and all the mentors and learners who have followed
a nonformal activity related programme.

Table of Contents

Introduction

This Home Learning Resource is a nonformal activity related learning programme, supporting learners to take control of their learning, guided by personal and activity mentors. It supports formal learning but does not produce an individual qualification. This home-learning process builds knowledge and skills that are transferrable.

The Learning Process

This simple model describes the planning and evaluation cycle. Central to all work is the process of activity related learning, which requires continuous needs analysis. Needs may be identified by learners themselves or they may be perceived by mentors. A mentor is a responsible adult, who can be family members, supervisors, trainers and coaches etc. Learners should be included throughout the process and particularly in the review stage.

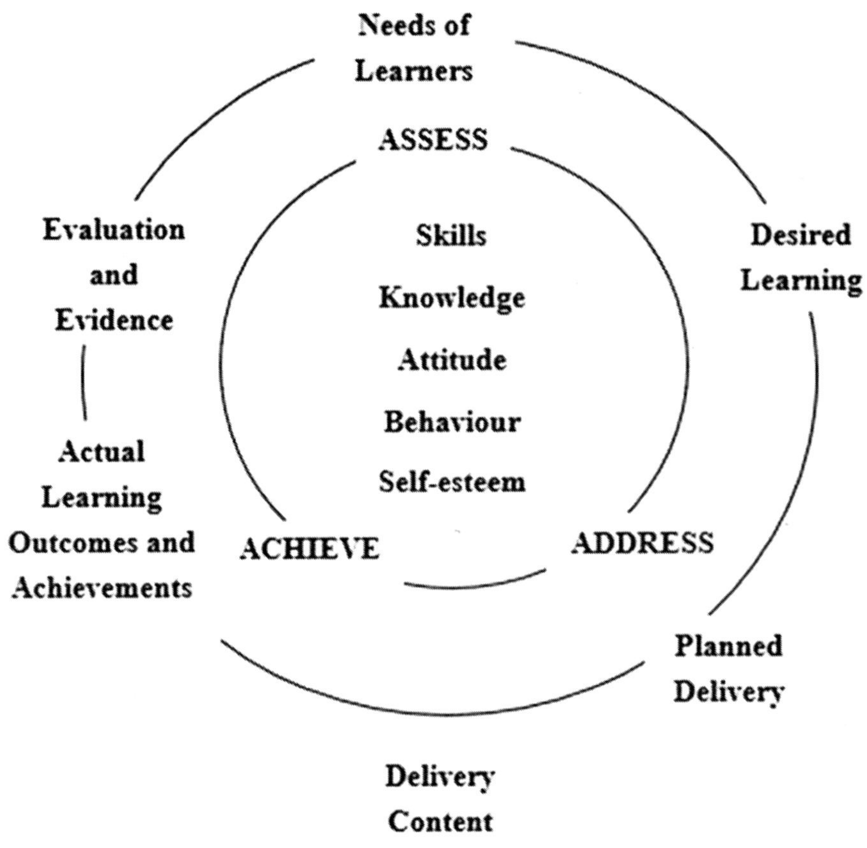

The Learner

The Learner can be any age and any gender.

Encouraging them to take progressively more responsibility for:

The Learner has the potential to succeed given the right opportunities. The key to success is to provide:

- Empathetic supportive mentors
- A structured activity focussed environment, which can develop a sense of belonging
- Experience of personal success
- Empowerment: taking increasing responsibility for activities, learning, self and other
- Personal development, including priority and other social skills.

Self-Esteem

- Experience success, counter past failure, and resist peer group pressure; an accurate self-image based on self-awareness; appropriate role modes
- A positive life-view, something to look forward to and work for, linked to motivation
- A commitment to control or change their lives (recognising that only they can do this, not being dependent on others, accepting that they themselves by their own effort can achieve a worthwhile future).

PERSONAL MENTOR

The role of the personal mentor—meeting learners' personal needs and maximising learning.

Personal Mentor Roles:

- Provide a safe environment
- Engender a sense of belonging
- Listen to their perception of reality
- Provide space for risk taking and discovery
- Engender trust and acceptance of students as they are
- Build confidence and self-worth (self-esteem)
- Encourage to explore feelings and hopes for the future
- Recognise and explore the values they are living by
- Help them plan and review their learning, and assess the learning outcomes
- Enable learner to build portfolios to support their learning.

Activity Mentor

The Activity Mentor has expertise in the activity being undertaken by the learner. They can be coaches, supervisors, trainers, leaders, and specialists, interested and knowledgeable adults. They will:
Provide a safe environment, a sense of partnership and belonging, someone to listen to and space for risk taking and personal discovery.

- Give the learner confidence.
- Engendering trust and acceptance of them as they are.
- Helping them to emphasise with the experience of others.
- Recognising and exploring the values they are living by.

Nonformal Learning

A DEFINITION OF NONFORMAL LEARNING

Education that is institutionalised, intentional and planned. The defining characteristic of nonformal education is that it is an addition, alternative and/or a complement to formal education within the process of the lifelong learning of individuals. It is often provided to guarantee the right of access to education for all. It caters for people of all ages. But does not necessarily apply a continuous pathway-structure; it may be short in duration and/or low intensity, and it is typically provided in the form of various activities. Nonformal education leads to qualifications that are not recognised as formal qualifications by the relevant national educational authorities. Nonformal education can cover programmes contributing to lifelong learning, as well as programmes on life skills, work skills, and social or cultural development.

Nonformal Learning

Formal educational systems alone cannot respond to the challenges of modern society and therefore needs reinforcement by nonformal learning practices. Nonformal learning must be a de facto partner in the lifelong learning process and make it accessible for all.

Coombes and Ahmed Definitions:

Formal Education

The highly institutionalised, chronologically graded and hierarchically structured 'education system' spanning primary school and the upper reaches of university.

Nonformal Learning

Any organised, systematic, educational activity carried on outside the framework of the formal system to provide selected types of learning to subgroups in the population, adults as well as young people.
Nonformal learning, delivered by nonformal educators (personal development and learning support mentors, activity mentors and any other appropriate and skilled adult).
To change their attitudes and behaviour, learner's needs can be summarised as:

- **Belonging**, feeling part of the learning provision
- **Priority social skills, and other social skills** necessary for successful learning
- **Partnership with the others working with them,** utilising learners as a major resource
- **Responsibility (empowerment)** through involvement in decision making
- **A relevant and appropriate curriculum**
- **Recognition of their achievements**

To do this, nonformal educators, as a starting point:

- Provide a safe environment.
- Provide a sense of partnership and belonging.
- Provide someone to listen to them.
- Provide space for risk taking and personal discovery.
- Give the learners confidence.
- Engender trust and acceptance of them as they are.
- Encourage them to explore and share feelings and hopes for the future.
- Help them emphasise with the experience of others.
- Recognise and explore the values they are living by.

Activity Related Learning

Implement Activity Related Learning That:

Is sensitive to the social characteristics which shape learners' lives.

Develop the social skills necessary to successfully implement their own decisions for their lives.

Enable them to take progressively more responsibility for their activities, their learning, themselves, and each other.

Develop learning outcomes and assessment criteria, which will equip them to become more skilled at interpersonal relationships, better self-starters, team-workers, problem-solvers, and independent learners.

Other Social Skills

- Recognising and managing feelings (impulse and anger control, develop alternative strategies for addressing conflict)
- Understand and identify with others—empathy (to recognise the feelings, needs and points of view of other students and mentors, or victims of crime)
- Values development (to identify, understand and explore alternatives to current values, beliefs and behaviour, and their consequences, particularly in relation to a lifelong learning ethos)

Employability Skills

- Positive attitude
- Social skills
- Willingness to learn
- Reliability
- Punctual
- Getting on with others
- Interested in the work
- Smart appearance
- Not require direct supervision
- Work hard on allocated tasks

Personal Development Objectives

Desired learning outcomes:

- Skills
- Knowledge
- Attitude
- Behaviour
- Self-esteem and confidence.

Basic Assumptions Underpinning the Curriculum

In any form of learning, it is important to recognise that learners are unique individuals with different needs, interests, abilities, and aspirations.

Central to the implementation of this framework is a relationship of trust, mutual respect, with time set aside to pay attention to the progress and achievement of each learner.

Learners benefit from having a mentor with whom they decide: the nature of the project or activity through which they will learn the combinations of outcomes they seek to achieve.

The mentor is an adult with whom they can develop a significant 'attachment'. Acting as guide and assessor, the mentor adds considerably to the value of the learning experience.

Curriculum Guidelines

- Encourage progressive responsibility and ownership of learning.
- Provide a mechanism by which to measure the quality of work.
- Reinforce good practice.
- Encourage participation and social inclusion.
- Use peer education if possible.
- Provide structured and broad open-ended challenges.

By empowering learners with a degree of choice of the many activities related learning opportunities, they develop a sense of ownership of the learning involved. This alone is highly motivating and is further advanced by a sense of achievement that recognises their individual contributions to the activities in which they are involved.
Nonformal Activity Related Learning Curriculum Framework

- Challenging Prejudice and Discrimination
- Citizenship and Community
- Creative and Expressive Arts
- Cultural Diversity and International Links
- Health and Survival
- Independent Living
- Personal and Interpersonal Skills
- Preparing for Work
- Sport and Leisure
- Personal Interests

THE LEARNER AND MENTOR SELECT THE TOPICS/CHALLENGES THEY WANT TO UNDERTAKE. THEY CAN DO AS MANY TOPICS/CHALLENGES AS THEY WANT. THEY DO NOT HAVE TO COMPLETE EVERY SECTION OR IN ANY ORDER.

Challenging Prejudice and Discrimination
Challenging Prejudice and Discrimination aims to work towards ensuring that everyone has equality of opportunity and is not disadvantaged because of the prejudicial views or discriminatory behaviour of others.
We recognise that by positively challenging prejudice and discrimination we will start process of change aimed at redressing the inequalities in society.

Desired Learning Outcomes Skills

Learners will be able/are developing the skills to:

- Challenge prejudice and discrimination.
- Accept, in a positive manner, challenges made by others regarding their own prejudices or discriminatory behaviour.
- Combat bullying.
- Take positive steps in response to challenge.
- Recognise the effects of prejudice and discrimination on their own lives and the lives of others.

Knowledge
Learners will have increased their knowledge/understand:

- All forms of prejudice and discrimination e.g. based upon race, gender, sexuality disability, appearance, lifestyle, beliefs.
- How people can be disadvantaged or excluded because of the views or actions of others.
- Different cultures, beliefs, backgrounds, and lifestyles
- What action they can take to challenge prejudice and discrimination and to combat inequalities.
- Local and national support structures for those who are victims of prejudice or discrimination.

Attitude
Learners will have changed/questioned their attitude regarding:

- What constitutes prejudice or discrimination
- The needs, rights and responsibilities of themselves and other people.
- The effects of peer pressure and influences upon their lives.
- Their personal responsibilities in challenging others and being open to challenge themselves.
- Action they can take to promote equality of opportunity.

Behaviour
Learners will have taken positive action to:

- Challenge prejudicial views and challenge discriminatory behaviour.
- Refrain themselves from expressing prejudicial views or behaving in a discriminatory manner.
- Promote positive peer interaction and support.
- Explore and gain greater understanding of the need of other people, their backgrounds and lifestyles.

Self-esteem and Confidence
Learners will have demonstrated that they have the self-esteem/confidence to:

- Value themselves, their background, beliefs and abilities.
- Challenge other people's views and actions.
- Be able to positively accept challenge themselves.
- Raise awareness with others.
- Work in partnership with others.

<table>
<tr><td>NAME</td><td colspan="7"></td></tr>
<tr><td>Date Started</td><td></td><td colspan="2">Date Completed</td><td colspan="4"></td></tr>
<tr><td colspan="8"></td></tr>
<tr><td rowspan="2">ACTIVITY</td><td colspan="3">Challenging Prejudice and Discrimination</td><td colspan="4" rowspan="2">SCORE</td></tr>
<tr><td colspan="3">Explore the issues around prejudice and discrimination</td></tr>
<tr><td colspan="4">Learners to understand: All forms of prejudice and discrimination, based upon race, gender, sexuality disability, appearance, lifestyle, beliefs.</td><td colspan="4">1 | 2 | 3 | 4 | 5</td></tr>
<tr><td colspan="4">How people can be disadvantaged or excluded because of the views or actions of others.</td><td colspan="4">1 | 2 | 3 | 4 | 5</td></tr>
<tr><td colspan="4">Explore and explain the different cultures, beliefs, backgrounds, and lifestyles.</td><td colspan="4">1 | 2 | 3 | 4 | 5</td></tr>
<tr><td colspan="4">Action that can be taken to promote equality of opportunity.</td><td colspan="4">1 | 2 | 3 | 4 | 5</td></tr>
<tr><td colspan="4">Explore and explain the local and national support structures for those who are victims of prejudice or discrimination.</td><td colspan="4">1 | 2 | 3 | 4 | 5</td></tr>
<tr><td>1</td><td>2</td><td>3</td><td>4</td><td colspan="4">5</td></tr>
<tr><td>Has no understanding at this level</td><td>Has little understanding at this level</td><td>Has some understanding at this level</td><td>Has a good understanding at this level</td><td colspan="4">Has knowledge beyond this level</td></tr>
<tr><td colspan="8">• Each element must score a 4 or 5 to achieve a pass mark at the level attempted.
• Each element can be attempted as many times as it is necessary to achieve the pass mark at the level attempted.
• On attainment of the required pass mark the evidence for each element is accepted as part of the profile.</td></tr>
<tr><td>Mentor/Witness Comments
Signature:</td><td colspan="7"></td></tr>
<tr><td>Learner Comments
Signature:</td><td colspan="7"></td></tr>
</table>

<table>
<tr><td>NAME</td><td colspan="7"></td></tr>
<tr><td>Date Started</td><td></td><td>Date Completed</td><td colspan="5"></td></tr>
<tr><td colspan="8"></td></tr>
<tr><td rowspan="2">ACTIVITY</td><td colspan="2">Challenging Prejudice and Discrimination</td><td colspan="5" rowspan="2">SCORE</td></tr>
<tr><td colspan="2">Race and ethnicity</td></tr>
<tr><td colspan="3">Explain the differences between race and ethnicity.</td><td>1</td><td>2</td><td>3</td><td>4</td><td>5</td></tr>
<tr><td colspan="3">Identify the different races in your community and the wider region.</td><td>1</td><td>2</td><td>3</td><td>4</td><td>5</td></tr>
<tr><td colspan="3">What are the benefits of a multi race community, and what are the negatives?</td><td>1</td><td>2</td><td>3</td><td>4</td><td>5</td></tr>
<tr><td colspan="3">Describe how ethnicity changes the culture of your community and wider region.</td><td>1</td><td>2</td><td>3</td><td>4</td><td>5</td></tr>
<tr><td colspan="3">Investigate your own ethnicity and that of your family.</td><td>1</td><td>2</td><td>3</td><td>4</td><td>5</td></tr>
</table>

<table>
<tr><td>1</td><td>2</td><td>3</td><td>4</td><td>5</td></tr>
<tr><td>Has no understanding at this level</td><td>Has little understanding at this level</td><td>Has some understanding at this level</td><td>Has a good understanding at this level</td><td>Has knowledge beyond this level</td></tr>
<tr><td colspan="5">

- Each element must score a 4 or 5 to achieve a pass mark at the level attempted.
- Each element can be attempted as many times as it is necessary to achieve the pass mark at the level attempted.
- On attainment of the required pass mark the evidence for each element is accepted as part of the profile.

</td></tr>
<tr><td>Mentor/Witness Comments
Signature:</td><td colspan="4"></td></tr>
<tr><td>Learner Comments
Signature:</td><td colspan="4"></td></tr>
</table>

<table>
<tr><td>NAME</td><td colspan="8"></td></tr>
<tr><td>Date Started</td><td></td><td>Date Completed</td><td colspan="6"></td></tr>
<tr><td colspan="9"></td></tr>
<tr><td rowspan="2">ACTIVITY</td><td colspan="3">Challenging Prejudice and Discrimination</td><td rowspan="2" colspan="5">SCORE</td></tr>
<tr><td colspan="3">Disability</td></tr>
<tr><td colspan="4">Explain the different forms of disability.</td><td>1</td><td>2</td><td>3</td><td>4</td><td>5</td></tr>
<tr><td colspan="4">How does a disability discriminate against the individual?</td><td>1</td><td>2</td><td>3</td><td>4</td><td>5</td></tr>
<tr><td colspan="4">How can society support the disabled?</td><td>1</td><td>2</td><td>3</td><td>4</td><td>5</td></tr>
<tr><td colspan="4">Name as many individuals as you can who have overcome a disability to achieve great success.</td><td>1</td><td>2</td><td>3</td><td>4</td><td>5</td></tr>
<tr><td colspan="4">How do you promote positive discrimination?</td><td>1</td><td>2</td><td>3</td><td>4</td><td>5</td></tr>
<tr><td>1</td><td>2</td><td>3</td><td>4</td><td colspan="5">5</td></tr>
<tr><td>Has no understanding at this level</td><td>Has little understanding at this level</td><td>Has some understanding at this level</td><td>Has a good understanding at this level</td><td colspan="5">Has knowledge beyond this level</td></tr>
<tr><td colspan="9"><ul><li>Each element must score a 4 or 5 to achieve a pass mark at the level attempted.</li><li>Each element can be attempted as many times as it is necessary to achieve the pass mark at the level attempted.</li><li>On attainment of the required pass mark the evidence for each element is accepted as part of the profile.</li></ul></td></tr>
<tr><td>Mentor/Witness Comments
Signature:</td><td colspan="8"></td></tr>
<tr><td>Learner Comments
Signature:</td><td colspan="8"></td></tr>
</table>

NAME				
Date Started		**Date Completed**		

ACTIVITY	Challenging Prejudice and Discrimination Bullying	SCORE				
Describe as many different aspects as possible of bullying you are aware of.		1	2	3	4	5
Describe your feelings about bullying that affects you and your friends.		1	2	3	4	5
How would you describe mental bullying?		1	2	3	4	5
What do you understand by online bullying?		1	2	3	4	5
How would you challenge and combat bullying?		1	2	3	4	5

1	2	3	4	5
Has no understanding at this level	**Has little understanding at this level**	**Has some understanding at this level**	**Has a good understanding at this level**	**Has knowledge beyond this level**

- Each element must score a 4 or 5 to achieve a pass mark at the level attempted.
- Each element can be attempted as many times as it is necessary to achieve the pass mark at the level attempted.
- On attainment of the required pass mark the evidence for each element is accepted as part of the profile.

Mentor/Witness Comments **Signature:**	
Learner Comments **Signature:**	

Each piece of evidence is ticked off from the evidence chart and filed/stored in your personal portfolio file

Evidence that shows the candidate:	Produced by the candidate:	Collected by the candidate:	Produced by others:
Was involved in the activity	• *Consent Forms* • *Leaflets* • *Booklets* • *Travel tickets* • *Events tickets* • *Events programme* • *Flyers* • *Maps* • *Course information* • *Newspaper cuttings* • *Certificates*	• *Photographs* • *Video recording* • *Audio recording* • *Activity Review Sheet* • *Arts Review Sheet* • *Finished piece of work* • *Drawings* • *Questionnaires* • *Letters* • *Emails* • *Phone records* • *Plans* • *Designs* • *Posters* • *Memos* • *Notices* • *Posters* • *Diary* • *Scripts*	• *Mentor* • *observations* • *Witness observations* • *Artist observations* • *Employer* • *Observations* • *Family observations* • *Peer observations*
Worked towards their targets	• *Certificates* • *Test results*	• *Questionnaires* • *Activity Review Sheet* • *Evaluation Forms* • *Feedback sessions* • *Diary/Logbook* • *Timelines*	• *Witness observations* • *Peer observations* • *Attendance records*
Took the appropriate amount of responsibility	• *Role descriptions* • *Work plans* • *Task Sheets* • *Diary* • *Logbook* • *Activity Review Sheet*	• *Role descriptions* • *Work plans* • *Task Sheets* • *Diary/Logbook* • *Activity Review Sheet*	

Citizenship and Community

Citizenship and Community aims to encourage learners to be part of their local communities. It is important that learners become informed citizens within their communities, developing awareness, participation, and responsibility for the positive contribution they can make.

We have a role to play in offering learners' opportunities to understand the political, economic, and social forces operating within their community and globally and how they can become involved in the process of change through participation and empowerment.

Desired Learning Outcomes

Skills

Learners will be able/are developing the skills to:

- Identify ways to help people in the community who have problems.
- Identify ways in which they can play an active part in their community.
- Contribute effectively to the democratic process.
- Understand the decision-making process at a local/national/international level.
- Make informed decisions about issues within their communities.
- Understand their rights and responsibilities within society.

Knowledge

Learners will have increased their knowledge/have an understanding of:

- Local/national/international political structures
- The democratic process and how they can engage with it
- Their rights and responsibilities within society
- What contribution they can make to their local community

Attitude

Learners will have changed/questioned their attitude regarding:

- How they might have a critical respect for other people's views.
- The need to be responsible for their own actions.
- Being a force for change within their own communities.
- What they as individuals can bring to their communities and society.

Behaviour

Learners will have taken positive action to:

- Consider what the issues are within their communities.
- Be responsible for their actions.
- Be viewed as positive role models within their communities.
- Work co-operatively with a range of people within their communities.
- Consider the needs of others within their community.

Self-Esteem and Confidence

Learners will have demonstrated that they have the self-esteem/confidence to:

- Listen to and accept the ideas of others
- Challenge other people's views and actions
- Exercise their rights and responsibilities
- Make suggestions that are relevant to the situation
- Make positive contributions to their community

<table>
<tr><td>NAME</td><td colspan="7"></td></tr>
<tr><td>Date Started</td><td></td><td>Date Completed</td><td colspan="5"></td></tr>
<tr><td colspan="8"></td></tr>
<tr><td rowspan="2">ACTIVITY</td><td colspan="2">Citizenship and Community</td><td colspan="5" rowspan="2">SCORE</td></tr>
<tr><td colspan="2">Managing your life</td></tr>
<tr><td colspan="3">Understand the structure of your family, extended family, and neighbourhood</td><td>1</td><td>2</td><td>3</td><td>4</td><td>5</td></tr>
<tr><td colspan="3">Develop an understanding of local government</td><td>1</td><td>2</td><td>3</td><td>4</td><td>5</td></tr>
<tr><td colspan="3">Develop an understanding of national government</td><td>1</td><td>2</td><td>3</td><td>4</td><td>5</td></tr>
<tr><td colspan="3">Develop an understanding of other countries systems of government</td><td>1</td><td>2</td><td>3</td><td>4</td><td>5</td></tr>
<tr><td colspan="3">Develop an understanding of world organisations which affect our lives</td><td>1</td><td>2</td><td>3</td><td>4</td><td>5</td></tr>
</table>

1	2	3	4	5
Has no understanding at this level	**Has little understanding at this level**	**Has some understanding at this level**	**Has a good understanding at this level**	**Has knowledge beyond this level**

- Each element must score a 4 or 5 to achieve a pass mark at the level attempted.
- Each element can be attempted as many times as it is necessary to achieve the pass mark at the level attempted.
- On attainment of the required pass mark the evidence for each element is accepted as part of the profile.

Mentor/Witness Comments **Signature:**	
Learner Comments **Signature:**	

<table>
<tr><td>NAME</td><td colspan="6"></td></tr>
<tr><td>Date Started</td><td></td><td>Date Completed</td><td colspan="5"></td></tr>
<tr><td colspan="8"></td></tr>
<tr><td rowspan="2">ACTIVITY</td><td colspan="2">Citizenship and Community</td><td colspan="5" rowspan="2">SCORE</td></tr>
<tr><td colspan="2">Rights and responsibilities</td></tr>
<tr><td colspan="3">Provide examples of your rights and responsibilities. Demonstrate how you balance your rights and responsibilities.</td><td>1</td><td>2</td><td>3</td><td>4</td><td>5</td></tr>
<tr><td colspan="3">Understand how your attitudes towards rights and responsibilities affect you and other.</td><td>1</td><td>2</td><td>3</td><td>4</td><td>5</td></tr>
<tr><td colspan="3">Think about the possible consequences of your actions.</td><td>1</td><td>2</td><td>3</td><td>4</td><td>5</td></tr>
<tr><td colspan="3">Give an example of a right and responsibility to do with: yourself, a parent, a partner, or as an employee.</td><td>1</td><td>2</td><td>3</td><td>4</td><td>5</td></tr>
<tr><td colspan="3">Describe the challenges you might face in exercising these rights and responsibilities if you were in each role and how you would tackle these challenges.</td><td>1</td><td>2</td><td>3</td><td>4</td><td>5</td></tr>
</table>

<table>
<tr><td>1</td><td>2</td><td>3</td><td>4</td><td>5</td></tr>
<tr><td>Has no understanding at this level</td><td>Has little understanding at this level</td><td>Has some understanding at this level</td><td>Has a good understanding at this level</td><td>Has knowledge beyond this level</td></tr>
<tr><td colspan="5">• Each element must score a 4 or 5 to achieve a pass mark at the level attempted.
• Each element can be attempted as many times as it is necessary to achieve the pass mark at the level attempted.
• On attainment of the required pass mark the evidence for each element is accepted as part of the profile.</td></tr>
<tr><td>Mentor/Witness Comments
Signature:</td><td colspan="4"></td></tr>
<tr><td>Learner Comments
Signature:</td><td colspan="4"></td></tr>
</table>

<table>
<tr><td>NAME</td><td colspan="8"></td></tr>
<tr><td>Date Started</td><td></td><td colspan="2">Date Completed</td><td colspan="5"></td></tr>
<tr><td colspan="9"></td></tr>
<tr><td rowspan="2">ACTIVITY</td><td colspan="3">Citizenship and Community</td><td colspan="5" rowspan="2">SCORE</td></tr>
<tr><td colspan="3">Manage your own commitment</td></tr>
<tr><td colspan="4">What part can you play in promoting local citizenship?</td><td>1</td><td>2</td><td>3</td><td>4</td><td>5</td></tr>
<tr><td colspan="4">Describe your own community and the role you play within it.</td><td>1</td><td>2</td><td>3</td><td>4</td><td>5</td></tr>
<tr><td colspan="4">What does be a good citizen mean?</td><td>1</td><td>2</td><td>3</td><td>4</td><td>5</td></tr>
<tr><td colspan="4">What does the Citizens Advice Bureau offer?</td><td>1</td><td>2</td><td>3</td><td>4</td><td>5</td></tr>
<tr><td colspan="4">How can you promote positive community action?</td><td>1</td><td>2</td><td>3</td><td>4</td><td>5</td></tr>
<tr><td>1</td><td>2</td><td>3</td><td>4</td><td colspan="5">5</td></tr>
<tr><td>Has no understanding at this level</td><td>Has little understanding at this level</td><td>Has some understanding at this level</td><td>Has a good understanding at this level</td><td colspan="5">Has knowledge beyond this level</td></tr>
<tr><td colspan="9">• Each element must score a 4 or 5 to achieve a pass mark at the level attempted.
• Each element can be attempted as many times as it is necessary to achieve the pass mark at the level attempted.
• On attainment of the required pass mark the evidence for each element is accepted as part of the profile.</td></tr>
<tr><td>Mentor/Witness Comments
Signature:</td><td colspan="8"></td></tr>
<tr><td>Learner Comments
Signature:</td><td colspan="8"></td></tr>
</table>

<table>
<tr><td>NAME</td><td colspan="7"></td></tr>
<tr><td>Date Started</td><td></td><td colspan="2">Date Completed</td><td colspan="5"></td></tr>
<tr><td colspan="9"></td></tr>
<tr><td rowspan="2">ACTIVITY</td><td colspan="3">Citizenship and Community</td><td rowspan="2" colspan="5">SCORE</td></tr>
<tr><td colspan="3">Have knowledge of internationalism</td></tr>
<tr><td colspan="4">What do you understand by internationalism?</td><td>1</td><td>2</td><td>3</td><td>4</td><td>5</td></tr>
<tr><td colspan="4">How can you promote internationalism for the positive?</td><td>1</td><td>2</td><td>3</td><td>4</td><td>5</td></tr>
<tr><td colspan="4">What international organisations are in your area?</td><td>1</td><td>2</td><td>3</td><td>4</td><td>5</td></tr>
<tr><td colspan="4">How can being an internationalist improve society?</td><td>1</td><td>2</td><td>3</td><td>4</td><td>5</td></tr>
<tr><td colspan="4">Describe the actions of international organisations.</td><td>1</td><td>2</td><td>3</td><td>4</td><td>5</td></tr>
<tr><td>1</td><td>2</td><td>3</td><td>4</td><td colspan="5">5</td></tr>
<tr><td>Has no understanding at this level</td><td>Has little understanding at this level</td><td>Has some understanding at this level</td><td>Has a good understanding at this level</td><td colspan="5">Has knowledge beyond this level</td></tr>
<tr><td colspan="9">• Each element must score a 4 or 5 to achieve a pass mark at the level attempted.
• Each element can be attempted as many times as it is necessary to achieve the pass mark at the level attempted.
• On attainment of the required pass mark the evidence for each element is accepted as part of the profile.</td></tr>
<tr><td>Mentor/Witness Comments
Signature:</td><td colspan="8"></td></tr>
<tr><td>Learner Comments
Signature:</td><td colspan="8"></td></tr>
</table>

Each piece of evidence is ticked off from the evidence chart and filed/stored in your personal portfolio file

Evidence that shows the candidate:	Produced by the candidate:	Collected by the candidate:	Produced by others:
Was involved in the activity	• *Photographs* • *Video recording* • *Audio recording* • *Activity Review Sheet* • *Arts Review Sheet* • *Finished piece of work* • *Drawings* • *Questionnaires* • *Letters* • *Emails* • *Phone records* • *Plans* • *Designs* • *Posters* • *Memos* • *Notices* • *Posters* • *Diary* • *Scripts*	• *Consent Forms* • *Leaflets* • *Booklets* • *Travel tickets* • *Events tickets* • *Events programme* • *Flyers* • *Maps* • *Course information* • *Newspaper cuttings* • *Certificates*	• *Mentor* • *observations* • *Witness observations* • *Artist observations* • *Employer* • *Observations* • *Family observations* • *Peer observations*
Worked towards their targets	• *Questionnaires* • *Activity Review Sheet* • *Evaluation Forms* • *Feedback sessions* • *Diary/Logbook* • *Timelines*	• *Certificates* • *Test results* • *Activity Review Sheet*	• *Witness observations* • *Peer observations* • *Attendance records*
Took the appropriate amount of responsibility	• *Role descriptions* • *Work plans* • *Task Sheets* • *Diary/Logbook* • *Activity Review Sheet*	• *Role descriptions* • *Work plans* • *Task Sheets* • *Diary/Logbook* • *Activity Review Sheet*	

Creative and Expressive Arts

Creative and Expressive Arts aims to provide learners with the opportunity to express themselves creatively and to participate in a range of art forms including visual arts, performing arts and crafts.
We will encourage creativity, expression, enjoyment, and social interaction through the arts.

Desired Learning Outcomes

Skills
Learners will be able/are developing the skills to:

- Utilise practical skills in:
  - Art
  - Craft
  - Dance
  - Drama
  - Music
  - Fashion
  - Literacy
  - Video and photography

- Express themselves creatively
- Interpret Creative and Expressive Arts work of others
- Address relevant issues through expressive art forms
- Plan, prepare for and execute a public performance or display

Knowledge
Learners will have increased their knowledge/have an understanding of:

- Different styles of Creative and Expressive Arts
- Creative and Expressive Arts which exists locally, regionally, nationally and internationally
- Educational and career opportunities in the field of Creative and Expressive Arts
- How Creative and Expressive Arts can be used to convey meaning, explore emotions and stimulate critical thinking.

Attitude
Learners will have changed/questioned their attitude regarding:

- How they might be involved in a range of art forms.
- Creative and Expressive Arts of cultures and historical periods.
- Creative and Expressive Arts as a means of self-expression and.
- Enjoyment.

Behaviour

Learners will have taken positive action to:

- Engage in a creative use of leisure time.
- Be creative and expressive as individuals.
- Be creative and expressive in a co-operative and collective manner
- Participate in an activity which challenges prejudice.

Self-Esteem and Confidence

Learners will have demonstrated that they have the self-esteem/confidence to:

- Express themselves as individuals.
- Express themselves in-group settings.
- Display their creative and expressive arts skills for others.
- Contribute ideas and challenge those of others.
- Listen to and accept the ideas of others.

<table>
<tr><td>NAME</td><td colspan="7"></td></tr>
<tr><td>Date Started</td><td></td><td colspan="2">Date Completed</td><td colspan="5"></td></tr>
<tr><td colspan="9"></td></tr>
<tr><td rowspan="2">ACTIVITY</td><td colspan="3">Creative and Expressive Arts</td><td rowspan="2" colspan="5">SCORE</td></tr>
<tr><td colspan="3">Music</td></tr>
<tr><td colspan="4">Try out a few musical instruments and select one in which you feel comfortable.</td><td>1</td><td>2</td><td>3</td><td>4</td><td>5</td></tr>
<tr><td colspan="4">Take lessons in your musical instrument of choice.</td><td>1</td><td>2</td><td>3</td><td>4</td><td>5</td></tr>
<tr><td colspan="4">Play solo showing your skills to an audience.</td><td>1</td><td>2</td><td>3</td><td>4</td><td>5</td></tr>
<tr><td colspan="4">Play in an ensemble or band.</td><td>1</td><td>2</td><td>3</td><td>4</td><td>5</td></tr>
<tr><td colspan="4">Give a performance or concert.</td><td>1</td><td>2</td><td>3</td><td>4</td><td>5</td></tr>
<tr><td>1</td><td>2</td><td>3</td><td>4</td><td colspan="5">5</td></tr>
<tr><td>Has no understanding at this level</td><td>Has little understanding at this level</td><td>Has some understanding at this level</td><td>Has a good understanding at this level</td><td colspan="5">Has knowledge beyond this level</td></tr>
<tr><td colspan="9">• Each element must score a 4 or 5 to achieve a pass mark at the level attempted.
• Each element can be attempted as many times as it is necessary to achieve the pass mark at the level attempted.
• On attainment of the required pass mark the evidence for each element is accepted as part of the profile.</td></tr>
<tr><td>Mentor/Witness Comments
Signature:</td><td colspan="8"></td></tr>
<tr><td>Learner Comments
Signature:</td><td colspan="8"></td></tr>
</table>

<table>
<tr><td>NAME</td><td colspan="7"></td></tr>
<tr><td>Date Started</td><td></td><td colspan="2">Date Completed</td><td colspan="4"></td></tr>
<tr><td colspan="8"></td></tr>
<tr><td rowspan="2">ACTIVITY</td><td colspan="2">Creative and Expressive Arts</td><td colspan="5" rowspan="2">SCORE</td></tr>
<tr><td colspan="2">Drama</td></tr>
<tr><td colspan="3">Visit a theatre and watch a performance.</td><td>1</td><td>2</td><td>3</td><td>4</td><td>5</td></tr>
<tr><td colspan="3">Attend drama lessons or a coaching course.</td><td>1</td><td>2</td><td>3</td><td>4</td><td>5</td></tr>
<tr><td colspan="3">Observe and comment on professional actors.</td><td>1</td><td>2</td><td>3</td><td>4</td><td>5</td></tr>
<tr><td colspan="3">Look at all openings for actors on stage, film, or video.</td><td>1</td><td>2</td><td>3</td><td>4</td><td>5</td></tr>
<tr><td colspan="3">Take part in a drama production.</td><td>1</td><td>2</td><td>3</td><td>4</td><td>5</td></tr>
</table>

<table>
<tr><td>1</td><td>2</td><td>3</td><td>4</td><td>5</td></tr>
<tr><td>Has no understanding at this level</td><td>Has little understanding at this level</td><td>Has some understanding at this level</td><td>Has a good understanding at this level</td><td>Has knowledge beyond this level</td></tr>
</table>

- Each element must score a 4 or 5 to achieve a pass mark at the level attempted.
- Each element can be attempted as many times as it is necessary to achieve the pass mark at the level attempted.
- On attainment of the required pass mark the evidence for each element is accepted as part of the profile.

Mentor/Witness Comments **Signature:**	
Learner Comments **Signature:**	

NAME				
Date Started		Date Completed		
ACTIVITY	Creative and Expressive Arts Drawing, Painting, Sculpture etc.		SCORE	

Activity					
Follow a sketching and drawing course of study.	1	2	3	4	5
Undertake a form of painting study, water colour, oil or any other form of painting.	1	2	3	4	5
Study one art form to a higher level.	1	2	3	4	5
Visit several art galleries and develop an understanding and knowledge of your taste in a particular art form.	1	2	3	4	5
Create your own exhibition.	1	2	3	4	5

1	2	3	4	5
Has no understanding at this level	**Has little understanding at this level**	**Has some understanding at this level**	**Has a good understanding at this level**	**Has knowledge beyond this level**

- Each element must score a 4 or 5 to achieve a pass mark at the level attempted.
- Each element can be attempted as many times as it is necessary to achieve the pass mark at the level attempted.
- On attainment of the required pass mark the evidence for each element is accepted as part of the profile.

Mentor/Witness Comments **Signature:**	
Learner Comments **Signature:**	

<table>
<tr><td>NAME</td><td colspan="8"></td></tr>
<tr><td>Date Started</td><td></td><td colspan="2">Date Completed</td><td colspan="5"></td></tr>
<tr><td colspan="9"></td></tr>
<tr><td rowspan="2">ACTIVITY</td><td colspan="3">Creative and Expressive Arts</td><td colspan="5" rowspan="2">SCORE</td></tr>
<tr><td colspan="3">Performance</td></tr>
<tr><td colspan="4">Describe as many different performances as possible.</td><td>1</td><td>2</td><td>3</td><td>4</td><td>5</td></tr>
<tr><td colspan="4">How can a multimedia performance be organised?</td><td>1</td><td>2</td><td>3</td><td>4</td><td>5</td></tr>
<tr><td colspan="4">Produce your own performance ideas in any genre you select.</td><td>1</td><td>2</td><td>3</td><td>4</td><td>5</td></tr>
<tr><td colspan="4">Give a detailed description of any performance you consider outstanding.</td><td>1</td><td>2</td><td>3</td><td>4</td><td>5</td></tr>
<tr><td colspan="4">Work with others and produce a collaborative performance.</td><td>1</td><td>2</td><td>3</td><td>4</td><td>5</td></tr>
<tr><td>1</td><td>2</td><td>3</td><td>4</td><td colspan="5">5</td></tr>
<tr><td>Has no understanding at this level</td><td>Has little understanding at this level</td><td>Has some understanding at this level</td><td>Has a good understanding at this level</td><td colspan="5">Has knowledge beyond this level</td></tr>
<tr><td colspan="9"><ul><li>Each element must score a 4 or 5 to achieve a pass mark at the level attempted.</li><li>Each element can be attempted as many times as it is necessary to achieve the pass mark at the level attempted.</li><li>On attainment of the required pass mark the evidence for each element is accepted as part of the profile.</li></ul></td></tr>
<tr><td>Mentor/Witness Comments
Signature:</td><td colspan="8"></td></tr>
<tr><td>Learner Comments
Signature:</td><td colspan="8"></td></tr>
</table>

Each piece of evidence is ticked off from the evidence chart and filed/stored in your personal portfolio file

Evidence that shows the candidate:	Produced by the candidate:	Collected by the candidate:	Produced by others:
Was involved in the activity	• *Photographs* • *Video recording* • *Audio recording* • *Activity Review Sheet* • *Arts Review Sheet* • *Finished piece of work* • *Drawings* • *Questionnaires* • *Letters* • *Emails* • *Phone records* • *Plans* • *Designs* • *Posters* • *Memos* • *Notices* • *Posters* • *Diary* • *Scripts*	• *Consent Forms* • *Leaflets* • *Booklets* • *Travel tickets* • *Events tickets* • *Events programme* • *Flyers* • *Maps* • *Course information* • *Newspaper cuttings* • *Certificates*	• *Mentor* • *observations* • *Witness observations* • *Artist observations* • *Employer* • *Observations* • *Family observations* • *Peer observations*
Worked towards their targets	• *Questionnaires* • *Activity Review Sheet* • *Evaluation Forms* • *Feedback sessions* • *Diary/Logbook* • *Timelines*	• *Certificates* • *Test results*	• *Witness observations* • *Peer observations* • *Attendance records*
Took the appropriate amount of responsibility	• *Role descriptions* • *Work plans* • *Task Sheets* • *Diary/Logbook* • *Activity Review Sheet*	• *Role descriptions* • *Work plans* • *Task Sheets* • *Diary/Logbook* • *Activity Review Sheet*	

Cultural Diversity and International Links

Cultural Diversity and International Links aims to provide learners with opportunities to explore, understand and appreciate different cultures and cultural experiences.
We have a role to play in making available a variety of cultural opportunities and experiences, which in widening horizons, will improve the quality of lives and understanding of cultural and community issues.

Desired Learning Outcomes

Skills
Learners will be able/are developing the skills to:

- Understand and appreciate cultural difference
- Demonstrate tolerance of difference
- Address relevant cross-cultural issues
- Work co-operatively with a range of people who are different from
- themselves
- Recognise the diversity of youth culture and its impact on society
- Understand their own culture and its impact on their values and
- Attitudes

Knowledge
Learners will have increased their knowledge/understanding:

- Different cultures and cross-cultural issues
- The rich cultural diversity in Britain and the wider world
- Where they can access information about different cultures
- How different cultural experiences can enrich people's lives

Attitude
Learners will have changed/questioned their attitude regarding:

- How they might be involved in a range of cultural experiences
- Cultures and religions other than their own
- Culture as a means of self-expression and enjoyment
- Respecting and valuing other cultures contribution to society
- Their views and opinions of other cultures

Behaviour
Learners will have taken positive action to:

- Challenge cultural intolerance
- Participate in cultural activities which positively challenge prejudice
- Work with others to effect change Value their own and a range of other cultures

Self-esteem and Confidence

Learners will have demonstrated that they have the self-esteem/confidence to:

- Listen to and accept the ideas of others
- Challenge other people's views and actions
- Meet and interact with people from other cultures
- Explore their own and others cultural differences
- Embrace cultural opportunities to raise their creative and
- Aesthetic aspirations

<table>
<tr><td>NAME</td><td colspan="5"></td></tr>
<tr><td>Date Started</td><td></td><td colspan="2">Date Completed</td><td colspan="2"></td></tr>
<tr><td colspan="6"></td></tr>
<tr><td rowspan="2">ACTIVITY</td><td colspan="3">Cultural Diversity and International Links</td><td colspan="2" rowspan="2">SCORE</td></tr>
<tr><td colspan="3">Have a knowledge of different cultures</td></tr>
<tr><td colspan="4">Describe the different cultures you are aware of.</td><td colspan="2">1 2 3 4 5</td></tr>
<tr><td colspan="4">What similarities are there between the various cultures?</td><td colspan="2">1 2 3 4 5</td></tr>
<tr><td colspan="4">What beliefs do individual cultures have?</td><td colspan="2">1 2 3 4 5</td></tr>
<tr><td colspan="4">Where do the different cultures exist around the world?</td><td colspan="2">1 2 3 4 5</td></tr>
<tr><td colspan="4">Explore ancient cultures.</td><td colspan="2">1 2 3 4 5</td></tr>
<tr><td>1</td><td>2</td><td>3</td><td>4</td><td colspan="2">5</td></tr>
<tr><td>Has no understanding at this level</td><td>Has little understanding at this level</td><td>Has some understanding at this level</td><td>Has a good understanding at this level</td><td colspan="2">Has knowledge beyond this level</td></tr>
<tr><td colspan="6">• Each element must score a 4 or 5 to achieve a pass mark at the level attempted.
• Each element can be attempted as many times as it is necessary to achieve the pass mark at the level attempted.
• On attainment of the required pass mark the evidence for each element is accepted as part of the profile.</td></tr>
<tr><td>Mentor/Witness Comments
Signature:</td><td colspan="5"></td></tr>
<tr><td>Learner Comments
Signature:</td><td colspan="5"></td></tr>
</table>

<table>
<tr><td>NAME</td><td colspan="7"></td></tr>
<tr><td>Date Started</td><td></td><td colspan="2">Date Completed</td><td colspan="4"></td></tr>
<tr><td colspan="8"></td></tr>
<tr><td rowspan="2">ACTIVITY</td><td colspan="3">Cultural Diversity and International Links</td><td colspan="4" rowspan="2">SCORE</td></tr>
<tr><td colspan="3">Cultural diversity where you live</td></tr>
<tr><td colspan="4">Describe the cultural diversity in your own community.</td><td>1</td><td>2</td><td>3</td><td>4</td><td>5</td></tr>
<tr><td colspan="4">How do you get involved in different cultures?</td><td>1</td><td>2</td><td>3</td><td>4</td><td>5</td></tr>
<tr><td colspan="4">How do different cultures enrich your life?</td><td>1</td><td>2</td><td>3</td><td>4</td><td>5</td></tr>
<tr><td colspan="4">Describe your own culture.</td><td>1</td><td>2</td><td>3</td><td>4</td><td>5</td></tr>
<tr><td colspan="4">What culture do you believe reflects your hopes for the future?</td><td>1</td><td>2</td><td>3</td><td>4</td><td>5</td></tr>
<tr><td>1</td><td>2</td><td>3</td><td>4</td><td colspan="5">5</td></tr>
<tr><td>Has no understanding at this level</td><td>Has little understanding at this level</td><td>Has some understanding at this level</td><td>Has a good understanding at this level</td><td colspan="5">Has knowledge beyond this level</td></tr>
<tr><td colspan="9">• Each element must score a 4 or 5 to achieve a pass mark at the level attempted.
• Each element can be attempted as many times as it is necessary to achieve the pass mark at the level attempted.
• On attainment of the required pass mark the evidence for each element is accepted as part of the profile.</td></tr>
<tr><td>Mentor/Witness Comments
Signature:</td><td colspan="8"></td></tr>
<tr><td>Learner Comments
Signature:</td><td colspan="8"></td></tr>
</table>

<table>
<tr><td>NAME</td><td colspan="8"></td></tr>
<tr><td>Date Started</td><td></td><td colspan="2">Date Completed</td><td colspan="5"></td></tr>
<tr><td colspan="9"></td></tr>
<tr><td rowspan="2">ACTIVITY</td><td colspan="3">Cultural Diversity and International Links</td><td colspan="5" rowspan="2">SCORE</td></tr>
<tr><td colspan="3">Language and culture</td></tr>
<tr><td colspan="4">Develop your skills in another language.</td><td>1</td><td>2</td><td>3</td><td>4</td><td>5</td></tr>
<tr><td colspan="4">Try out your new language skills by visiting another country.</td><td>1</td><td>2</td><td>3</td><td>4</td><td>5</td></tr>
<tr><td colspan="4">Describe the different culture of the country you are visiting.</td><td>1</td><td>2</td><td>3</td><td>4</td><td>5</td></tr>
<tr><td colspan="4">Travel around several countries and develop your language skills further.</td><td>1</td><td>2</td><td>3</td><td>4</td><td>5</td></tr>
<tr><td colspan="4">Understand the culture through language in the different countries.</td><td>1</td><td>2</td><td>3</td><td>4</td><td>5</td></tr>
<tr><td>1</td><td>2</td><td>3</td><td>4</td><td colspan="5">5</td></tr>
<tr><td>Has no understanding at this level</td><td>Has little understanding at this level</td><td>Has some understanding at this level</td><td>Has a good understanding at this level</td><td colspan="5">Has knowledge beyond this level</td></tr>
<tr><td colspan="9">• Each element must score a 4 or 5 to achieve a pass mark at the level attempted.
• Each element can be attempted as many times as it is necessary to achieve the pass mark at the level attempted.
• On attainment of the required pass mark the evidence for each element is accepted as part of the profile.</td></tr>
<tr><td>Mentor/Witness Comments
Signature:</td><td colspan="8"></td></tr>
<tr><td>Learner Comments
Signature:</td><td colspan="8"></td></tr>
</table>

<table>
<tr><td>NAME</td><td colspan="5"></td></tr>
<tr><td>Date Started</td><td colspan="2"></td><td colspan="2">Date Completed</td><td></td></tr>
<tr><td colspan="6"></td></tr>
<tr><td rowspan="2">ACTIVITY</td><td colspan="4">Cultural Diversity and International Links</td><td rowspan="2">SCORE</td></tr>
<tr><td colspan="4">International organisations</td></tr>
<tr><td colspan="5">List national organisations with international links.</td><td>1 2 3 4 5</td></tr>
<tr><td colspan="5">Outline the work of OXFAM.</td><td>1 2 3 4 5</td></tr>
<tr><td colspan="5">Outline the work of UNESCO.</td><td>1 2 3 4 5</td></tr>
<tr><td colspan="5">How did Live Aid change the world?</td><td>1 2 3 4 5</td></tr>
<tr><td colspan="5">Research the United Nations.</td><td>1 2 3 4 5</td></tr>
<tr><td>1</td><td>2</td><td>3</td><td colspan="2">4</td><td>5</td></tr>
<tr><td>Has no understanding at this level</td><td>Has little understanding at this level</td><td>Has some understanding at this level</td><td colspan="2">Has a good understanding at this level</td><td>Has knowledge beyond this level</td></tr>
<tr><td colspan="6">• Each element must score a 4 or 5 to achieve a pass mark at the level attempted.
• Each element can be attempted as many times as it is necessary to achieve the pass mark at the level attempted.
• On attainment of the required pass mark the evidence for each element is accepted as part of the profile.</td></tr>
<tr><td>Mentor/Witness Comments
Signature:</td><td colspan="5"></td></tr>
<tr><td>Learner Comments
Signature:</td><td colspan="5"></td></tr>
</table>

Each piece of evidence is ticked off from the evidence chart and filed/stored in your personal portfolio file

Evidence that shows the candidate:	**Produced by the candidate:**	**Collected by the candidate:**	**Produced by others:**
Was involved in the activity	• *Photographs* • *Video recording* • *Audio recording* • *Activity Review Sheet* • *Arts Review Sheet* • *Finished piece of work* • *Drawings* • *Questionnaires* • *Letters* • *Emails* • *Phone records* • *Plans* • *Designs* • *Posters* • *Memos* • *Notices* • *Posters* • *Diary* • *Scripts*	• *Consent Forms* • *Leaflets* • *Booklets* • *Travel tickets* • *Events tickets* • *Events programme* • *Flyers* • *Maps* • *Course information* • *Newspaper cuttings* • *Certificates*	• *Mentor* • *observations* • *Witness observations* • *Artist observations* • *Employer* • *Observations* • *Family observations* • *Peer observations*
Worked towards their targets	• *Questionnaires* • *Activity Review Sheet* • *Evaluation Forms* • *Feedback sessions* • *Diary/Logbook* • *Timelines*	• *Certificates* • *Test results*	• *Witness observations* • *Peer observations* • *Attendance records*
Took the appropriate amount of responsibility	• *Role descriptions* • *Work plans* • *Task Sheets* • *Diary/Logbook* • *Activity Review Sheet*	• *Role descriptions* • *Work plans* • *Task Sheets* • *Diary/Logbook* • *Activity Review Sheet*	

Health and Survival

Healthy and Survival aims to encompass an approach in offering a 'holistic' way of working with learners around specific health issues, which affect their physical, spiritual, emotional, and mental well-being.
The Personal Curriculum can provide settings and opportunities in which issues relating to healthy living can be raised, enabling learners to make informed decisions about their health, their relationships and their lifestyle.

Desired Learning Outcomes

Skills
Learners will be able/are developing the skills to:

- Share their views and talk with others
- Manage their emotions
- Talk about personal feelings
- Make use of information available
- Assess their own needs
- Assess needs of others

Knowledge
Learners will have increased their knowledge/understand:

- How to access relevant and up-to-date information
- Consequences relating to drugs and other substance misuse
- How to access support services and health facilities available to all
- Their rights in relation to health matters
- The risks involved in certain actions
- A wide range of health-related issues

Attitude
Learners will have changed/questioned their attitude regarding:

- Taking personal responsibility for their well being
- Taking responsibility for the wellbeing of others
- How health issues affect their lives
- Their views and opinions towards health issues

Behaviour
Learners will have taken positive action to:

- Make informed choices about their lifestyle
- Adopt a healthier lifestyle
- Act assertively when making health decisions
- Assess their needs and respond appropriately
- Assessing the needs of others and responding appropriately

Self-esteem and Confidence

Learners will have demonstrated that they have the self-esteem/confidence to:

- Develop a feeling of self-worth as a basis for adopting a healthier lifestyle
- Take pride in their own appearance and in maintaining a healthy
- lifestyle
- Make decisions and choices in their own best interests
- Have a positive self-image and feel good about themselves
- Resist unwanted peer pressure

<table>
<tr><td>NAME</td><td colspan="7"></td></tr>
<tr><td>Date Started</td><td></td><td colspan="2">Date Completed</td><td colspan="4"></td></tr>
<tr><td colspan="8"></td></tr>
<tr><td rowspan="2">ACTIVITY</td><td colspan="3">Health and Survival</td><td colspan="4" rowspan="2">SCORE</td></tr>
<tr><td colspan="3">Wellbeing and lifestyle</td></tr>
<tr><td colspan="4">How would you describe wellbeing and lifestyle?</td><td>1</td><td>2</td><td>3</td><td>4 5</td></tr>
<tr><td colspan="4">Does wellbeing affect your lifestyle?</td><td>1</td><td>2</td><td>3</td><td>4 5</td></tr>
<tr><td colspan="4">What is good mental wellbeing and what is poor mental wellbeing?</td><td>1</td><td>2</td><td>3</td><td>4 5</td></tr>
<tr><td colspan="4">How can you improve your mental wellbeing?</td><td>1</td><td>2</td><td>3</td><td>4 5</td></tr>
<tr><td colspan="4">How can you improve your own wellbeing and lifestyle?</td><td>1</td><td>2</td><td>3</td><td>4 5</td></tr>
<tr><td>1</td><td>2</td><td>3</td><td>4</td><td colspan="4">5</td></tr>
<tr><td>Has no understanding at this level</td><td>Has little understanding at this level</td><td>Has some understanding at this level</td><td>Has a good understanding at this level</td><td colspan="4">Has knowledge beyond this level</td></tr>
<tr><td colspan="8">• Each element must score a 4 or 5 to achieve a pass mark at the level attempted.
• Each element can be attempted as many times as it is necessary to achieve the pass mark at the level attempted.
• On attainment of the required pass mark the evidence for each element is accepted as part of the profile.</td></tr>
<tr><td>Mentor/Witness Comments
Signature:</td><td colspan="7"></td></tr>
<tr><td>Learner Comments
Signature:</td><td colspan="7"></td></tr>
</table>

NAME							
Date Started		Date Completed					
ACTIVITY	Health and Survival Services		SCORE				
What health services are available for your community?			1	2	3	4	5
How do national health services impact on your life?			1	2	3	4	5
How would you improve your health support system?			1	2	3	4	5
How can private healthcare and the national health service work together?			1	2	3	4	5
How is your healthcare funded?			1	2	3	4	5

1	2	3	4	5
Has no understanding at this level	**Has little understanding at this level**	**Has some understanding at this level**	**Has a good understanding at this level**	**Has knowledge beyond this level**

- Each element must score a 4 or 5 to achieve a pass mark at the level attempted.
- Each element can be attempted as many times as it is necessary to achieve the pass mark at the level attempted.
- On attainment of the required pass mark the evidence for each element is accepted as part of the profile.

Mentor/Witness Comments **Signature:**	
Learner Comments **Signature:**	

NAME			
Date Started		**Date Completed**	

ACTIVITY	Health and Survival Drugs and solvent abuse	SCORE				
List the legal drugs that are available to you, prescription or otherwise.		1	2	3	4	5
List the illegal drugs you are aware of.		1	2	3	4	5
Would you decriminalise certain illegal drugs?		1	2	3	4	5
What assistance is available for excessive drug users?		1	2	3	4	5
Prepare a campaign with a strong anti-drug message?		1	2	3	4	5

1	2	3	4	5
Has no understanding at this level	**Has little understanding at this level**	**Has some understanding at this level**	**Has a good understanding at this level**	**Has knowledge beyond this level**

- Each element must score a 4 or 5 to achieve a pass mark at the level attempted.
- Each element can be attempted as many times as it is necessary to achieve the pass mark at the level attempted.
- On attainment of the required pass mark the evidence for each element is accepted as part of the profile.

Mentor/Witness Comments **Signature:**	
Learner Comments **Signature:**	

<table>
<tr><td>NAME</td><td colspan="7"></td></tr>
<tr><td>Date Started</td><td></td><td>Date Completed</td><td colspan="5"></td></tr>
<tr><td colspan="8"></td></tr>
<tr><td rowspan="2">ACTIVITY</td><td colspan="2">Health and Survival</td><td colspan="5" rowspan="2">SCORE</td></tr>
<tr><td colspan="2">Positive health action</td></tr>
<tr><td colspan="3">Devise a healthy eating programme'</td><td>1</td><td>2</td><td>3</td><td>4</td><td>5</td></tr>
<tr><td colspan="3">Devise a healthy lifestyle programme.</td><td>1</td><td>2</td><td>3</td><td>4</td><td>5</td></tr>
<tr><td colspan="3">How can you monitor your health?</td><td>1</td><td>2</td><td>3</td><td>4</td><td>5</td></tr>
<tr><td colspan="3">Does family health history affect your own health?</td><td>1</td><td>2</td><td>3</td><td>4</td><td>5</td></tr>
<tr><td colspan="3">How can you get involved with improving the health of your community?</td><td>1</td><td>2</td><td>3</td><td>4</td><td>5</td></tr>
</table>

<table>
<tr><td>1</td><td>2</td><td>3</td><td>4</td><td>5</td></tr>
<tr><td>Has no understanding at this level</td><td>Has little understanding at this level</td><td>Has some understanding at this level</td><td>Has a good understanding at this level</td><td>Has knowledge beyond this level</td></tr>
<tr><td colspan="5">
• Each element must score a 4 or 5 to achieve a pass mark at the level attempted.
• Each element can be attempted as many times as it is necessary to achieve the pass mark at the level attempted.
• On attainment of the required pass mark the evidence for each element is accepted as part of the profile.
</td></tr>
<tr><td>Mentor/Witness Comments
Signature:</td><td colspan="4"></td></tr>
<tr><td>Learner Comments
Signature:</td><td colspan="4"></td></tr>
</table>

Each piece of evidence is ticked off from the evidence chart and filed/stored in your personal portfolio file

Evidence that shows the candidate:	Produced by the candidate:	Collected by the candidate:	Produced by others:
Was involved in the activity	• *Photographs* • *Video recording* • *Audio recording* • *Activity Review Sheet* • *Arts Review Sheet* • *Finished piece of work* • *Drawings* • *Questionnaires* • *Letters* • *Emails* • *Phone records* • *Plans* • *Designs* • *Posters* • *Memos* • *Notices* • *Posters* • *Diary* • *Scripts*	• *Consent Forms* • *Leaflets* • *Booklets* • *Travel tickets* • *Events tickets* • *Events programme* • *Flyers* • *Maps* • *Course information* • *Newspaper cuttings* • *Certificates*	• *Mentor* • *observations* • *Witness observations* • *Artist observations* • *Employer* • *Observations* • *Family observations* • *Peer observations*
Worked towards their targets	• *Questionnaires* • *Activity Review Sheet* • *Evaluation Forms* • *Feedback sessions* • *Diary/Logbook* • *Timelines*	• *Certificates* • *Test results*	• *Witness observations* • *Peer observations* • *Attendance records*
Took the appropriate amount of responsibility	• *Role descriptions* • *Work plans* • *Task Sheets* • *Diary/Logbook* • *Activity Review Sheet*	• *Role descriptions* • *Work plans* • *Task Sheets* • *Diary/Logbook* • *Activity Review Sheet*	

Independent Living

Independent Living aims to enable and support learners towards living independently.
We will support learners for this any stage in their lives, and to explore the options open to them and to make informed choices about their future, examining practical issues and problems they may face.

Desired Learning Outcomes

Skills

- Learners will be able/are developing skills to:
- Identify hazards and risks in their personal environment
- Demonstrate a range of practical skills associated with independent living
- Identify a range of people who can offer support and information
- Explore the issues associated with living independently
- Talk to agencies about future options
- Resolve conflict

Knowledge

Learners will have increased their knowledge/have an understanding of:

- What options are available to learners
- What are their rights and responsibilities
- What are the issues relating to independent living
- What are the legal issues relevant to independent living
- What agencies can support them

Attitude

Learners will have changed/questioned their attitude regarding:

- Asking for support from others
- What support is needed when making the transition to living
- independently
- Taking personal responsibility
- Other views of learners living independently
- Resolving problems and conflict.

Behaviour

Learners will have taken positive action to:

- Identify personal values and how they affect behaviour
- Negotiate, compromise, and resolve problems
- Assess the impact of own behaviour on others
- Challenge prejudice and stereotyping
- Manage themselves effectively

Self-Esteem and Confidence

Learners will have demonstrated that they have the self-esteem/confidence to:

- Feel positive about choices that they make
- Deal with the issues of independent living
- Recognise and learn from their mistakes
- Contribute to the process of identifying their own strengths and weaknesses
- Respond constructively to feedback

<table>
<tr><td>NAME</td><td colspan="8"></td></tr>
<tr><td>Date Started</td><td></td><td colspan="2">Date Completed</td><td colspan="5"></td></tr>
<tr><td colspan="9"></td></tr>
<tr><td rowspan="2">ACTIVITY</td><td colspan="3">Independent Living</td><td colspan="5" rowspan="2">SCORE</td></tr>
<tr><td colspan="3">Living accommodation</td></tr>
<tr><td colspan="4">Search for location, apartments, flats, houses, or shared accommodation to your choice.</td><td>1</td><td>2</td><td>3</td><td>4</td><td>5</td></tr>
<tr><td colspan="4">Look carefully at your moving costs.</td><td>1</td><td>2</td><td>3</td><td>4</td><td>5</td></tr>
<tr><td colspan="4">What is the maintenance of your home entail?</td><td>1</td><td>2</td><td>3</td><td>4</td><td>5</td></tr>
<tr><td colspan="4">Plan and undertake a DIY project in your new home.</td><td>1</td><td>2</td><td>3</td><td>4</td><td>5</td></tr>
<tr><td colspan="4">What transport needs do you have for your new accommodation?</td><td>1</td><td>2</td><td>3</td><td>4</td><td>5</td></tr>
<tr><td>1</td><td>2</td><td>3</td><td>4</td><td colspan="5">5</td></tr>
<tr><td>Has no understanding at this level</td><td>Has little understanding at this level</td><td>Has some understanding at this level</td><td>Has a good understanding at this level</td><td colspan="5">Has knowledge beyond this level</td></tr>
<tr><td colspan="9">• Each element must score a 4 or 5 to achieve a pass mark at the level attempted.
• Each element can be attempted as many times as it is necessary to achieve the pass mark at the level attempted.
• On attainment of the required pass mark the evidence for each element is accepted as part of the profile.</td></tr>
<tr><td>Mentor/Witness Comments
Signature:</td><td colspan="8"></td></tr>
<tr><td>Learner Comments
Signature:</td><td colspan="8"></td></tr>
</table>

<table>
<tr><td>NAME</td><td colspan="7"></td></tr>
<tr><td>Date Started</td><td></td><td colspan="2">Date Completed</td><td colspan="4"></td></tr>
<tr><td colspan="8"></td></tr>
<tr><td rowspan="2">ACTIVITY</td><td colspan="3">Independent Living</td><td colspan="4" rowspan="2">SCORE</td></tr>
<tr><td colspan="3">Furnishing your home</td></tr>
<tr><td colspan="4">Plan the furniture required for each room in your home.</td><td>1</td><td>2</td><td>3</td><td>4</td><td>5</td></tr>
<tr><td colspan="4">Search catalogues and shops for your requirements.</td><td>1</td><td>2</td><td>3</td><td>4</td><td>5</td></tr>
<tr><td colspan="4">Compare the cost of your items and compare it with your budget, modify your purchases accordingly.</td><td>1</td><td>2</td><td>3</td><td>4</td><td>5</td></tr>
<tr><td colspan="4">Search charity shops for alternatives and ask friends and family for hand me downs.</td><td>1</td><td>2</td><td>3</td><td>4</td><td>5</td></tr>
<tr><td colspan="4">Identify the décor you want for your new home, cost of materials and application.</td><td>1</td><td>2</td><td>3</td><td>4</td><td>5</td></tr>
<tr><td>1</td><td>2</td><td>3</td><td>4</td><td colspan="5">5</td></tr>
<tr><td>Has no understanding at this level</td><td>Has little understanding at this level</td><td>Has some understanding at this level</td><td>Has a good understanding at this level</td><td colspan="5">Has knowledge beyond this level</td></tr>
<tr><td colspan="9">
<ul>
<li>Each element must score a 4 or 5 to achieve a pass mark at the level attempted.</li>
<li>Each element can be attempted as many times as it is necessary to achieve the pass mark at the level attempted.</li>
<li>On attainment of the required pass mark the evidence for each element is accepted as part of the profile.</li>
</ul>
</td></tr>
<tr><td>Mentor/Witness Comments
Signature:</td><td colspan="8"></td></tr>
<tr><td>Learner Comments
Signature:</td><td colspan="8"></td></tr>
</table>

<table>
<tr><td>NAME</td><td colspan="5"></td></tr>
<tr><td>Date Started</td><td></td><td colspan="2">Date Completed</td><td colspan="2"></td></tr>
<tr><td colspan="6"></td></tr>
<tr><td rowspan="2">ACTIVITY</td><td colspan="3">Independent Living</td><td colspan="2" rowspan="2">SCORE</td></tr>
<tr><td colspan="3">Paying the bills</td></tr>
</table>

Activity					
Outline all the utility bills you will have to pay and add up your approximate total cost.	**1**	**2**	**3**	**4**	**5**
Outline the remaining household bills you must pay and add up your approximate cost	**1**	**2**	**3**	**4**	**5**
How can you reduce your bills?	**1**	**2**	**3**	**4**	**5**
What different methods can you find to pay all your bills?	**1**	**2**	**3**	**4**	**5**
How will you budget for all your living costs?	**1**	**2**	**3**	**4**	**5**

1	2	3	4	5
Has no understanding at this level	**Has little understanding at this level**	**Has some understanding at this level**	**Has a good understanding at this level**	**Has knowledge beyond this level**

- Each element must score a 4 or 5 to achieve a pass mark at the level attempted.
- Each element can be attempted as many times as it is necessary to achieve the pass mark at the level attempted.
- On attainment of the required pass mark the evidence for each element is accepted as part of the profile.

Mentor/Witness Comments **Signature:**	
Learner Comments **Signature:**	

<table>
<tr><td>NAME</td><td colspan="4"></td></tr>
<tr><td>Date Started</td><td></td><td>Date Completed</td><td colspan="2"></td></tr>
<tr><td colspan="5"></td></tr>
<tr><td rowspan="2">ACTIVITY</td><td colspan="3">Independent Living</td><td rowspan="2">SCORE</td></tr>
<tr><td colspan="3">Feeding Yourself</td></tr>
<tr><td colspan="4">Prepare a balances menu for the week and budget the costs.</td><td>1 2 3 4 5</td></tr>
<tr><td colspan="4">Shop for the ingredients you will use for your meals.</td><td>1 2 3 4 5</td></tr>
<tr><td colspan="4">Cook the meals each day and rate them accordingly.</td><td>1 2 3 4 5</td></tr>
<tr><td colspan="4">Bake a celebration cake.</td><td>1 2 3 4 5</td></tr>
<tr><td colspan="4">Prepare a special meal for friends or family.</td><td>1 2 3 4 5</td></tr>
<tr><td>1</td><td>2</td><td>3</td><td>4</td><td>5</td></tr>
<tr><td>Has no understanding at this level</td><td>Has little understanding at this level</td><td>Has some understanding at this level</td><td>Has a good understanding at this level</td><td>Has knowledge beyond this level</td></tr>
<tr><td colspan="5">• Each element must score a 4 or 5 to achieve a pass mark at the level attempted.
• Each element can be attempted as many times as it is necessary to achieve the pass mark at the level attempted.
• On attainment of the required pass mark the evidence for each element is accepted as part of the profile.</td></tr>
<tr><td>Mentor/Witness Comments
Signature:</td><td colspan="4"></td></tr>
<tr><td>Learner Comments
Signature:</td><td colspan="4"></td></tr>
</table>

Personal and Interpersonal Skills

Personal and Interpersonal Development aims to enable learners to reach their full potential as individuals and positively interact with others.
We will provide opportunities and settings where learners are encouraged to develop their social skills, build relationships, communicate, listen, make decisions, and understand. The individual and collective needs of learners and the issucs affccting them are the focus for all activities.

Desired Learning Outcomes

Skills
Learners will be able/are developing skills to:

- (Personal) negotiate
- Manage aggression
- Observe
- Make decisions
- Understand
- (Communicate) listen
- Respond appropriately to others
- Express a point of view clearly
- Disagree and challenge others constructively
- (Group skills) abide by the democratic decisions of the group
- "Agree to disagree"
- Respect the views and thought of others

Knowledge

- How to communicate with others
- Different forms human communication takes (e.g., verbal, non-verbal)
- How others may perceive them because of their actions
- Potential positive benefits of co-operating with others
- How their actions affect others

Attitude
Learners will have changed/questioned their attitude regarding:

- Respecting themselves and others
- Taking pride in their achievements and successes
- Respecting the views of others

Behaviour
Learners will have taken positive action to:

- Act in a collective and co-operative manner
- Be more considerate towards the needs of others
- Be more tolerant towards the views and values of others
- Work with others to effect change.

Self-Esteem and Confidence

Learners will have demonstrated that they have the self-esteem/confidence to:

- Value what they themselves believe and value
- Express their beliefs and values in a variety of ways
- Express themselves as an individual
- Express themselves in group settings
- Participate in activities
- Participate constructively in group settings

NAME				
Date Started		Date Completed		

ACTIVITY	Personal and Interpersonal Skills Communication	SCORE				
Explain and explore verbal communication.		1	2	3	4	5
Explain and explore nonverbal communication.		1	2	3	4	5
Have the capability to learn, write and converse		1	2	3	4	5
How do you communicate with other different cultures and languages?		1	2	3	4	5
Learn sign language and communicate with the deaf.		1	2	3	4	5

1	2	3	4	5
Has no understanding at this level	**Has little understanding at this level**	**Has some understanding at this level**	**Has a good understanding at this level**	**Has knowledge beyond this level**

- Each element must score a 4 or 5 to achieve a pass mark at the level attempted.
- Each element can be attempted as many times as it is necessary to achieve the pass mark at the level attempted.
- On attainment of the required pass mark the evidence for each element is accepted as part of the profile.

Mentor/Witness Comments **Signature:**	
Learner Comments **Signature:**	

<table>
<tr><td colspan="2">NAME</td><td colspan="6"></td></tr>
<tr><td>Date Started</td><td></td><td>Date Completed</td><td colspan="5"></td></tr>
<tr><td colspan="8"></td></tr>
<tr><td rowspan="2">ACTIVITY</td><td colspan="2">Personal and Interpersonal Skills</td><td colspan="5" rowspan="2">SCORE</td></tr>
<tr><td colspan="2">Leadership</td></tr>
<tr><td colspan="3">Self-awareness is the foundation of a good leader. Do you understand what leadership style works best for you?</td><td>1</td><td>2</td><td>3</td><td>4</td><td>5</td></tr>
<tr><td colspan="3">Know the difference between delegating styles and which one is appropriate for each situation.</td><td>1</td><td>2</td><td>3</td><td>4</td><td>5</td></tr>
<tr><td colspan="3">In what situation do you play a leadership role?</td><td>1</td><td>2</td><td>3</td><td>4</td><td>5</td></tr>
<tr><td colspan="3">Name significant leaders that have affected your life and you consider them role models.</td><td>1</td><td>2</td><td>3</td><td>4</td><td>5</td></tr>
<tr><td colspan="3">Describe the qualities of a good leader.</td><td>1</td><td>2</td><td>3</td><td>4</td><td>5</td></tr>
</table>

1	2	3	4	5
Has no understanding at this level	**Has little understanding at this level**	**Has some understanding at this level**	**Has a good understanding at this level**	**Has knowledge beyond this level**

- Each element must score a 4 or 5 to achieve a pass mark at the level attempted.
- Each element can be attempted as many times as it is necessary to achieve the pass mark at the level attempted.
- On attainment of the required pass mark the evidence for each element is accepted as part of the profile.

Mentor/Witness Comments **Signature:**	
Learner Comments **Signature:**	

<table>
<tr><td>NAME</td><td colspan="7"></td></tr>
<tr><td>Date Started</td><td></td><td colspan="2">Date Completed</td><td colspan="5"></td></tr>
<tr><td colspan="9"></td></tr>
<tr><td rowspan="2">ACTIVITY</td><td colspan="3">Personal and Interpersonal Skills</td><td colspan="5" rowspan="2">SCORE</td></tr>
<tr><td colspan="3">Team building</td></tr>
<tr><td colspan="4">What do you know about team building?</td><td>1</td><td>2</td><td>3</td><td>4</td><td>5</td></tr>
<tr><td colspan="4">Experience a team building experience.</td><td>1</td><td>2</td><td>3</td><td>4</td><td>5</td></tr>
<tr><td colspan="4">Develop a team building programme based on outside activities.</td><td>1</td><td>2</td><td>3</td><td>4</td><td>5</td></tr>
<tr><td colspan="4">How would you use a team building experience to improve the standards of the work force?</td><td>1</td><td>2</td><td>3</td><td>4</td><td>5</td></tr>
<tr><td colspan="4">In what circumstances would you apply a team building programme?</td><td>1</td><td>2</td><td>3</td><td>4</td><td>5</td></tr>
<tr><td>1</td><td>2</td><td>3</td><td>4</td><td colspan="5">5</td></tr>
<tr><td>Has no understanding at this level</td><td>Has little understanding at this level</td><td>Has some understanding at this level</td><td>Has a good understanding at this level</td><td colspan="5">Has knowledge beyond this level</td></tr>
<tr><td colspan="9">
• Each element must score a 4 or 5 to achieve a pass mark at the level attempted.
• Each element can be attempted as many times as it is necessary to achieve the pass mark at the level attempted.
• On attainment of the required pass mark the evidence for each element is accepted as part of the profile.
</td></tr>
<tr><td>Mentor/Witness Comments
Signature:</td><td colspan="8"></td></tr>
<tr><td>Learner Comments
Signature:</td><td colspan="8"></td></tr>
</table>

<table>
<tr><td>NAME</td><td colspan="7"></td></tr>
<tr><td>Date Started</td><td></td><td colspan="2">Date Completed</td><td colspan="4"></td></tr>
<tr><td colspan="8"></td></tr>
<tr><td rowspan="2">ACTIVITY</td><td colspan="3">Personal and Interpersonal Skills</td><td colspan="4" rowspan="2">SCORE</td></tr>
<tr><td colspan="3">Computer Knowledge</td></tr>
<tr><td colspan="4">Have a basic understanding of personal computer packages such as Microsoft Office.</td><td>1</td><td>2</td><td>3</td><td>4 5</td></tr>
<tr><td colspan="4">Have abilities in web navigation, social media websites, and email methods.</td><td>1</td><td>2</td><td>3</td><td>4 5</td></tr>
<tr><td colspan="4">How can you use the internet safely?</td><td>1</td><td>2</td><td>3</td><td>4 5</td></tr>
<tr><td colspan="4">Use the web to research a project of your choice.</td><td>1</td><td>2</td><td>3</td><td>4 5</td></tr>
<tr><td colspan="4">Outline and develop a website for your family.</td><td>1</td><td>2</td><td>3</td><td>4 5</td></tr>
<tr><td>1</td><td>2</td><td>3</td><td>4</td><td colspan="4">5</td></tr>
<tr><td>Has no understanding at this level</td><td>Has little understanding at this level</td><td>Has some understanding at this level</td><td>Has a good understanding at this level</td><td colspan="4">Has knowledge beyond this level</td></tr>
<tr><td colspan="8">
<ul>
<li>Each element must score a 4 or 5 to achieve a pass mark at the level attempted.</li>
<li>Each element can be attempted as many times as it is necessary to achieve the pass mark at the level attempted.</li>
<li>On attainment of the required pass mark the evidence for each element is accepted as part of the profile.</li>
</ul>
</td></tr>
<tr><td>Mentor/Witness Comments
Signature:</td><td colspan="7"></td></tr>
<tr><td>Learner Comments
Signature:</td><td colspan="7"></td></tr>
</table>

Each piece of evidence is ticked off from the evidence chart and filed/stored in your personal portfolio file

Evidence that shows the candidate:	**Produced by the candidate:**	**Collected by the candidate:**	**Produced by others:**
Was involved in the activity	• *Photographs* • *Video recording* • *Audio recording* • *Activity Review Sheet* • *Arts Review Sheet* • *Finished piece of work* • *Drawings* • *Questionnaires* • *Letters* • *Emails* • *Phone records* • *Plans* • *Designs* • *Posters* • *Memos* • *Notices* • *Posters* • *Diary* • *Scripts*	• *Consent Forms* • *Leaflets* • *Booklets* • *Travel tickets* • *Events tickets* • *Events programme* • *Flyers* • *Maps* • *Course information* • *Newspaper cuttings* • *Certificates*	• *Mentor* • *observations* • *Witness observations* • *Artist observations* • *Employer* • *Observations* • *Family observations* • *Peer observations*
Worked towards their targets	• *Questionnaires* • *Activity Review Sheet* • *Evaluation Forms* • *Feedback sessions* • *Diary/Logbook* • *Timelines*	• *Certificates* • *Test results*	• *Witness observations* • *Peer observations* • *Attendance records*
Took the appropriate amount of responsibility	• *Role descriptions* • *Work plans* • *Task Sheets* • *Diary/Logbook* • *Activity Review Sheet*	• *Role descriptions* • *Work plans* • *Task Sheets* • *Diary* • *Logbook* • *Activity Review Sheet*	

Sport and Leisure

Sports and Leisure aims to encourage physical, spiritual, emotional and mental development. It is recognised that learners voluntarily participate in their leisure time and look for opportunities to engage in sporting and recreational pursuits.

We have a role to play in offering opportunities that enable learners to use sports and recreation as a positive vehicle for developing relationships, trust, mutual support, and friendship, whilst encouraging every individual to achieve their full potential.

The variety of opportunities available to mentors will enable imaginative development of learners and often can measure personal improvement and give recognition of achievement through local and national certification and awards.

Desired Learning Outcomes

Skills

Learners will be able/are developing skills to:

- Co-operate effectively with others
- Become effective team members
- Motivate others
- Demonstrate decision making skills
- Follow instructions effectively
- Further individual ability and talent
- Express themselves creatively

Knowledge

Learners will have increased their knowledge/have an understanding of:

- How to use their leisure time positively
- The benefits of a healthy and active lifestyle
- Where to find opportunities to pursue sporting and recreational activities
- How physical and mental activity lead to personal well being
- Rules related to their chosen sport or activity
- How to access information on sporting and recreational activities.

Attitude

Learners will have changed/questioned their attitude regarding:

- Taking part in activities which challenge them
- Tolerance towards others in a range of situations
- Having a responsible attitude towards self and others
- Fair play and acceptance of rules
- Health issues in relation to physical and mental activities.

Behaviour

Learners will have taken positive action to:

- Challenge aggression in sports
- Show respect for others involved in activity
- Assess the impact of own behaviour on others
- Act in an assertive not aggressive manner

Self-Esteem and Confidence

Learners will have demonstrated that they have the self-esteem/confidence to:

- Attain achievements which are recognised through awards and certification
- Pass on their skills to other clients
- Express themselves as individuals
- Express themselves in a group setting
- Positively accept challenge themselves

<table>
<tr><td>NAME</td><td colspan="7"></td></tr>
<tr><td>Date Started</td><td></td><td>Date Completed</td><td colspan="5"></td></tr>
<tr><td colspan="8"></td></tr>
<tr><td rowspan="2">ACTIVITY</td><td colspan="2">Sport and Leisure</td><td colspan="5" rowspan="2">SCORE</td></tr>
<tr><td colspan="2">Ball games without other equipment</td></tr>
<tr><td colspan="3">Try several of the following sports such as ~ football, basketball, netball, volleyball, rugby, handball, or other ball games played without equipment</td><td>1</td><td>2</td><td>3</td><td>4</td><td>5</td></tr>
<tr><td colspan="3">Choose two sports and attend coaching sessions</td><td>1</td><td>2</td><td>3</td><td>4</td><td>5</td></tr>
<tr><td colspan="3">Learn the rules of your chosen sport</td><td>1</td><td>2</td><td>3</td><td>4</td><td>5</td></tr>
<tr><td colspan="3">Play your chosen sports in games with other people</td><td>1</td><td>2</td><td>3</td><td>4</td><td>5</td></tr>
<tr><td colspan="3">Play your chosen sports in competitive games</td><td>1</td><td>2</td><td>3</td><td>4</td><td>5</td></tr>
</table>

<table>
<tr><td>1</td><td>2</td><td>3</td><td>4</td><td>5</td></tr>
<tr><td>Has no understanding at this level</td><td>Has little understanding at this level</td><td>Has some understanding at this level</td><td>Has a good understanding at this level</td><td>Has knowledge beyond this level</td></tr>
</table>

- Each element must score a 4 or 5 to achieve a pass mark at the level attempted.
- Each element can be attempted as many times as it is necessary to achieve the pass mark at the level attempted.
- On attainment of the required pass mark the evidence for each element is accepted as part of the profile.

<table>
<tr><td>Mentor/Witness Comments
Signature:</td><td></td></tr>
<tr><td>Learner Comments
Signature:</td><td></td></tr>
</table>

<table>
<tr><td>NAME</td><td colspan="7"></td></tr>
<tr><td>Date Started</td><td></td><td>Date Completed</td><td colspan="5"></td></tr>
<tr><td colspan="8"></td></tr>
<tr><td rowspan="2">ACTIVITY</td><td colspan="2">Sport and Leisure</td><td colspan="5" rowspan="2">SCORE</td></tr>
<tr><td colspan="2">Ball games with equipment</td></tr>
<tr><td colspan="3">Try several of the following sports such as ~ tennis, table tennis, hockey, golf, or other ball games played with equipment</td><td>1</td><td>2</td><td>3</td><td>4</td><td>5</td></tr>
<tr><td colspan="3">Choose two sports and attend coaching sessions</td><td>1</td><td>2</td><td>3</td><td>4</td><td>5</td></tr>
<tr><td colspan="3">Learn the rules of your chosen sport</td><td>1</td><td>2</td><td>3</td><td>4</td><td>5</td></tr>
<tr><td colspan="3">Play your chosen sports in games with other people</td><td>1</td><td>2</td><td>3</td><td>4</td><td>5</td></tr>
<tr><td colspan="3">Play your chosen sports in competitive games</td><td>1</td><td>2</td><td>3</td><td>4</td><td>5</td></tr>
</table>

<table>
<tr><td>1</td><td>2</td><td>3</td><td>4</td><td>5</td></tr>
<tr><td>Has no understanding at this level</td><td>Has little understanding at this level</td><td>Has some understanding at this level</td><td>Has a good understanding at this level</td><td>Has knowledge beyond this level</td></tr>
</table>

- Each element must score a 4 or 5 to achieve a pass mark at the level attempted.
- Each element can be attempted as many times as it is necessary to achieve the pass mark at the level attempted.
- On attainment of the required pass mark the evidence for each element is accepted as part of the profile.

Mentor/Witness Comments **Signature:**	
Learner Comments **Signature:**	

<table>
<tr><td>NAME</td><td colspan="7"></td></tr>
<tr><td>Date Started</td><td></td><td colspan="2">Date Completed</td><td colspan="4"></td></tr>
<tr><td colspan="8"></td></tr>
<tr><td rowspan="2">ACTIVITY</td><td colspan="2">Sport and Leisure</td><td colspan="5" rowspan="2">SCORE</td></tr>
<tr><td colspan="2">Keep fit exercising</td></tr>
<tr><td colspan="3">Study fitness in a sport of your choice and learn about the training programme and special diet involved.</td><td>1</td><td>2</td><td>3</td><td>4</td><td>5</td></tr>
<tr><td colspan="3">Plan a daily routine of keep fit exercises.</td><td>1</td><td>2</td><td>3</td><td>4</td><td>5</td></tr>
<tr><td colspan="3">Undertake walking, jogging, or running for fitness.</td><td>1</td><td>2</td><td>3</td><td>4</td><td>5</td></tr>
<tr><td colspan="3">Install fitness apparatus in your own home and exercise on a regular basis.</td><td>1</td><td>2</td><td>3</td><td>4</td><td>5</td></tr>
<tr><td colspan="3">Join a gym of your choice and follow a course of exercises.</td><td>1</td><td>2</td><td>3</td><td>4</td><td>5</td></tr>
<tr><td>1</td><td>2</td><td>3</td><td>4</td><td colspan="4">5</td></tr>
<tr><td>Has no understanding at this level</td><td>Has little understanding at this level</td><td>Has some understanding at this level</td><td>Has a good understanding at this level</td><td colspan="4">Has knowledge beyond this level</td></tr>
<tr><td colspan="8"><ul><li>Each element must score a 4 or 5 to achieve a pass mark at the level attempted.</li><li>Each element can be attempted as many times as it is necessary to achieve the pass mark at the level attempted.</li><li>On attainment of the required pass mark the evidence for each element is accepted as part of the profile.</li></ul></td></tr>
<tr><td>Mentor/Witness Comments
Signature:</td><td colspan="7"></td></tr>
<tr><td>Learner Comments
Signature:</td><td colspan="7"></td></tr>
</table>

<table>
<tr><td>NAME</td><td colspan="7"></td></tr>
<tr><td>Date Started</td><td></td><td colspan="2">Date Completed</td><td colspan="4"></td></tr>
<tr><td colspan="8"></td></tr>
<tr><td rowspan="2">ACTIVITY</td><td colspan="2">Sport and Leisure</td><td colspan="5" rowspan="2">SCORE</td></tr>
<tr><td colspan="2">The Olympics</td></tr>
<tr><td colspan="3">Explore the history of the Olympic Games Paralympics and also the Winter Olympics.</td><td>1</td><td>2</td><td>3</td><td>4</td><td>5</td></tr>
<tr><td colspan="3">Make a list of events in the Olympic Games, Paralympics and the Winter Olympics.</td><td>1</td><td>2</td><td>3</td><td>4</td><td>5</td></tr>
<tr><td colspan="3">Select three events from the Games and study them in depth.</td><td>1</td><td>2</td><td>3</td><td>4</td><td>5</td></tr>
<tr><td colspan="3">Choose an event you would like to compete in and prepare a training programme.</td><td>1</td><td>2</td><td>3</td><td>4</td><td>5</td></tr>
<tr><td colspan="3">Train for your chosen event and join a club or group to prepare for competition.</td><td>1</td><td>2</td><td>3</td><td>4</td><td>5</td></tr>
</table>

1	2	3	4	5
Has no understanding at this level	**Has little understanding at this level**	**Has some understanding at this level**	**Has a good understanding at this level**	**Has knowledge beyond this level**

- Each element must score a 4 or 5 to achieve a pass mark at the level attempted.
- Each element can be attempted as many times as it is necessary to achieve the pass mark at the level attempted.
- On attainment of the required pass mark the evidence for each element is accepted as part of the profile.

Mentor/Witness Comments **Signature:**	
Learner Comments **Signature:**	

Each piece of evidence is ticked off from the evidence chart and filed/stored in your personal portfolio file

Evidence that shows the candidate:	Produced by the candidate:	Collected by the candidate:	Produced by others:
Was involved in the activity	• *Photographs* • *Video recording* • *Audio recording* • *Activity Review Sheet* • *Arts Review Sheet* • *Finished piece of work* • *Drawings* • *Questionnaires* • *Letters* • *Emails* • *Phone records* • *Plans* • *Designs* • *Posters* • *Memos* • *Notices* • *Posters* • *Diary* • *Scripts*	• *Consent Forms* • *Leaflets* • *Booklets* • *Travel tickets* • *Events tickets* • *Events programme* • *Flyers* • *Maps* • *Course information* • *Newspaper cuttings* • *Certificates*	• *Mentor* • *observations* • *Witness observations* • *Artist observations* • *Employer* • *Observations* • *Family observations* • *Peer observations*
Worked towards their targets	• *Questionnaires* • *Activity Review Sheet* • *Evaluation Forms* • *Feedback sessions* • *Diary/Logbook* • *Timelines*	• *Certificates* • *Test results*	• *Witness observations* • *Peer observations* • *Attendance records*
Took the appropriate amount of responsibility	• *Role descriptions* • *Work plans* • *Task Sheets* • *Diary/Logbook* • *Activity Review Sheet*	• *Role descriptions* • *Work plans* • *Task Sheets* • *Diary* • *Logbook* • *Activity Review Sheet*	

Personal Interests

Personal Interests can be anything. Whatever the learner wants to explore and investigate further. Here are a few ideas.

- Amateur astronomy: You are patient, determined and detail-oriented.
- Amateur radio: You're creative and able to work to deadlines.
- Animals and pets: If you have several pets, you could apply your love for furry, feathered or scaly animals in a job as a pet sitter or veterinarian.
- Archery: You're focused and precise.
- Backgammon: You enjoy thinking strategically.
- Blogging: You have excellent planning and communication skills. (Don't forget to include a link to your blog but remember: no personal blogs!)
- Board games: You're a strategic thinker and a problem-solver.
- Bodybuilding: You're focused and self-disciplined.
- Calligraphy: You strive for perfection.
- Car restoration: You have excellent problem-solving and engineering skills.
- Chess: You're intelligent, analytical and good at developing business strategies.
- Childcare: You're a responsible individual.
- Club leadership: You are passionate, take initiative and have excellent interpersonal skills.
- Coding/Programming: You have strong analytical skills and the desire to learn.
- Collecting: You have a strong attention to detail, and you're passionate about your personal interests. Sadly, 'compulsively collecting cats' is discouraged.
- Cooking: You're creative and an excellent improviser.
- Crafts: This shows your intelligence and flair.
- Creative writing: You're imaginative. Use this for editorial positions or social media roles.
- Crossword puzzles: You have a broad vocabulary and may make a great writer.
- Do it yourself projects
- Fishing: You are patient and focused.
- Gardening: You care about nature and the environment, and this can effectively give you an advantage over the other candidates if you're seeking a role in sustainability and clean energy.
- Genealogy: You have strong research skills.
- Hiking: You're focused, and you have a clear head.
- Investing: You have strong planning skills, and you take risks.
- Jigsaw puzzles: You have excellent problem-solving skills.
- Knitting: You're a great multitasker and have strong planning skills.
- Landscaping: You are detail-oriented and an excellent planner.
- Languages: You appreciate diversity and have a keenness for culture.
- Lego building: You're patient, dexterous, imaginative, and a problem-solver.
- Martial arts: You have discipline and humility and are focused and confident.
- Meditation: You are calm and collected and have self-discipline.
- Model building: You're patient and detail oriented.
- Mountain biking: You're highly competitive and determined.
- Mountain climbing: You're focused and driven. This may help you enter the travel industry if you have no direct experience.
- Online classes: You're passionate about learning.
- Origami: You're creative and a problem-solver.

- Papermaking: You have a strong attention to detail, and you're creative.
- Parachuting: You take calculated risks.
- Paragliding: You have tenacity and drive.
- Reading: You have a thirst for knowledge, a particular passion for a subject matter, and you may make a great researcher.
- Recycling: This demonstrates environmental responsibility.
- Robotics: Technology driven.
- Rock climbing: You are purposeful and have strong problem-solving and interpersonal skills.
- Sailing: You are precise and assertive.
- Skiing: You're physically fit, and you have perseverance and excellent spatial reasoning skills.
- Skydiving: You push boundaries and take risk.
- Snooker/Pool: You have strong strategic and analytical skills.
- Surfing: You're proficient in assessing your immediate environment, while you're also a risk-taker.
- Travelling: Visiting different countries and exploring the world is seen as a valuable life experience. It shows that you have an appreciation for other cultures, and it helps you broaden your horizons.
- Video games: You're focused and determined.
- Video production: You're precise, focused and detail oriented.
- Volunteering: You work well with other people, and you're altruistic.
- Woodworking: You're confident, and you have a vision.
- Yoga: You're calm and in control. This makes you an attractive candidate if you're seeking a role in a busy and fast-paced environment.

<table>
<tr><td>NAME</td><td colspan="8"></td></tr>
<tr><td>Date Started</td><td></td><td colspan="2">Date Completed</td><td colspan="5"></td></tr>
<tr><td colspan="9"></td></tr>
<tr><td rowspan="2">ACTIVITY</td><td colspan="3">Personal Interests</td><td colspan="5" rowspan="2">SCORE</td></tr>
<tr><td colspan="3"></td></tr>
<tr><td colspan="4"></td><td>1</td><td>2</td><td>3</td><td>4</td><td>5</td></tr>
<tr><td colspan="4"></td><td>1</td><td>2</td><td>3</td><td>4</td><td>5</td></tr>
<tr><td colspan="4"></td><td>1</td><td>2</td><td>3</td><td>4</td><td>5</td></tr>
<tr><td colspan="4"></td><td>1</td><td>2</td><td>3</td><td>4</td><td>5</td></tr>
<tr><td colspan="4"></td><td>1</td><td>2</td><td>3</td><td>4</td><td>5</td></tr>
<tr><td>1</td><td>2</td><td>3</td><td>4</td><td colspan="5">5</td></tr>
<tr><td>Has no understanding at this level</td><td>Has little understanding at this level</td><td>Has some understanding at this level</td><td>Has a good understanding at this level</td><td colspan="5">Has knowledge beyond this level</td></tr>
<tr><td colspan="9">• Each element must score a 4 or 5 to achieve a pass mark at the level attempted.
• Each element can be attempted as many times as it is necessary to achieve the pass mark at the level attempted.
• On attainment of the required pass mark the evidence for each element is accepted as part of the profile.</td></tr>
<tr><td>Mentor/Witness Comments
Signature:</td><td colspan="8"></td></tr>
<tr><td>Learner Comments
Signature:</td><td colspan="8"></td></tr>
</table>

<table>
<tr><td>NAME</td><td colspan="7"></td></tr>
<tr><td>Date Started</td><td></td><td colspan="2">Date Completed</td><td colspan="4"></td></tr>
<tr><td colspan="8"></td></tr>
<tr><td rowspan="2">ACTIVITY</td><td colspan="3">Personal Interests</td><td colspan="4" rowspan="2">SCORE</td></tr>
<tr><td colspan="3"></td></tr>
<tr><td colspan="4"></td><td>1</td><td>2</td><td>3</td><td>4</td><td>5</td></tr>
<tr><td colspan="4"></td><td>1</td><td>2</td><td>3</td><td>4</td><td>5</td></tr>
<tr><td colspan="4"></td><td>1</td><td>2</td><td>3</td><td>4</td><td>5</td></tr>
<tr><td colspan="4"></td><td>1</td><td>2</td><td>3</td><td>4</td><td>5</td></tr>
<tr><td colspan="4"></td><td>1</td><td>2</td><td>3</td><td>4</td><td>5</td></tr>
<tr><td>1</td><td>2</td><td>3</td><td>4</td><td colspan="5">5</td></tr>
<tr><td>Has no understanding at this level</td><td>Has little understanding at this level</td><td>Has some understanding at this level</td><td>Has a good understanding at this level</td><td colspan="5">Has knowledge beyond this level</td></tr>
<tr><td colspan="9">• Each element must score a 4 or 5 to achieve a pass mark at the level attempted.
• Each element can be attempted as many times as it is necessary to achieve the pass mark at the level attempted.
• On attainment of the required pass mark the evidence for each element is accepted as part of the profile.</td></tr>
<tr><td>Mentor/Witness Comments
Signature:</td><td colspan="8"></td></tr>
<tr><td>Learner Comments
Signature:</td><td colspan="8"></td></tr>
</table>

<table>
<tr><td colspan="2">NAME</td><td colspan="7"></td></tr>
<tr><td colspan="2">Date Started</td><td></td><td>Date Cómpleted</td><td colspan="5"></td></tr>
<tr><td colspan="9"></td></tr>
<tr><td colspan="2" rowspan="2">ACTIVITY</td><td colspan="2">Personal Interests</td><td colspan="5" rowspan="2">SCORE</td></tr>
<tr><td colspan="2"></td></tr>
<tr><td colspan="4"></td><td>1</td><td>2</td><td>3</td><td>4</td><td>5</td></tr>
<tr><td colspan="4"></td><td>1</td><td>2</td><td>3</td><td>4</td><td>5</td></tr>
<tr><td colspan="4"></td><td>1</td><td>2</td><td>3</td><td>4</td><td>5</td></tr>
<tr><td colspan="4"></td><td>1</td><td>2</td><td>3</td><td>4</td><td>5</td></tr>
<tr><td colspan="4"></td><td>1</td><td>2</td><td>3</td><td>4</td><td>5</td></tr>
<tr><td colspan="2">1</td><td>2</td><td>3</td><td>4</td><td colspan="4">5</td></tr>
<tr><td colspan="2">Has no understanding at this level</td><td>Has little understanding at this level</td><td>Has some understanding at this level</td><td>Has a good understanding at this level</td><td colspan="4">Has knowledge beyond this level</td></tr>
<tr><td colspan="9">• Each element must score a 4 or 5 to achieve a pass mark at the level attempted.
• Each element can be attempted as many times as it is necessary to achieve the pass mark at the level attempted.
• On attainment of the required pass mark the evidence for each element is accepted as part of the profile.</td></tr>
<tr><td>Mentor/Witness Comments
Signature:</td><td colspan="8"></td></tr>
<tr><td>Learner Comments
Signature:</td><td colspan="8"></td></tr>
</table>

<table>
<tr><td colspan="2">NAME</td><td colspan="7"></td></tr>
<tr><td>Date Started</td><td></td><td colspan="2">Date Completed</td><td colspan="5"></td></tr>
<tr><td colspan="9"></td></tr>
<tr><td rowspan="2">ACTIVITY</td><td colspan="3">Personal Interests</td><td colspan="5" rowspan="2">SCORE</td></tr>
<tr><td colspan="3"></td></tr>
<tr><td colspan="4"></td><td>1</td><td>2</td><td>3</td><td>4</td><td>5</td></tr>
<tr><td colspan="4"></td><td>1</td><td>2</td><td>3</td><td>4</td><td>5</td></tr>
<tr><td colspan="4"></td><td>1</td><td>2</td><td>3</td><td>4</td><td>5</td></tr>
<tr><td colspan="4"></td><td>1</td><td>2</td><td>3</td><td>4</td><td>5</td></tr>
<tr><td colspan="4"></td><td>1</td><td>2</td><td>3</td><td>4</td><td>5</td></tr>
<tr><td>1</td><td>2</td><td>3</td><td>4</td><td colspan="5">5</td></tr>
<tr><td>Has no understanding at this level</td><td>Has little understanding at this level</td><td>Has some understanding at this level</td><td>Has a good understanding at this level</td><td colspan="5">Has knowledge beyond this level</td></tr>
<tr><td colspan="9"><ul><li>Each element must score a 4 or 5 to achieve a pass mark at the level attempted.</li><li>Each element can be attempted as many times as it is necessary to achieve the pass mark at the level attempted.</li><li>On attainment of the required pass mark the evidence for each element is accepted as part of the profile.</li></ul></td></tr>
<tr><td>Mentor/Witness Comments
Signature:</td><td colspan="8"></td></tr>
<tr><td>Learner Comments
Signature:</td><td colspan="8"></td></tr>
</table>

NAME								
Date Started		Date Completed						
ACTIVITY	Personal Interests		SCORE					
			1	2	3	4	5	
			1	2	3	4	5	
			1	2	3	4	5	
			1	2	3	4	5	
			1	2	3	4	5	

1	2	3	4	5
Has no understanding at this level	**Has little understanding at this level**	**Has some understanding at this level**	**Has a good understanding at this level**	**Has knowledge beyond this level**

- Each element must score a 4 or 5 to achieve a pass mark at the level attempted.
- Each element can be attempted as many times as it is necessary to achieve the pass mark at the level attempted.
- On attainment of the required pass mark the evidence for each element is accepted as part of the profile.

Mentor/Witness Comments **Signature:**	
Learner Comments **Signature:**	

Each piece of evidence is ticked off from the evidence chart and filed/stored in your personal portfolio file

Evidence that shows the candidate:	Produced by the candidate:	Collected by the candidate:	Produced by others:
Was involved in the activity	• *Photographs* • *Video recording* • *Audio recording* • *Activity Review Sheet* • *Arts Review Sheet* • *Finished piece of work* • *Drawings* • *Questionnaires* • *Letters* • *Emails* • *Phone records* • *Plans* • *Designs* • *Posters* • *Memos* • *Notices* • *Posters* • *Diary* • *Scripts*	• *Consent Forms* • *Leaflets* • *Booklets* • *Travel tickets* • *Events tickets* • *Events programme* • *Flyers* • *Maps* • *Course information* • *Newspaper cuttings* • *Certificates*	• *Mentor* • *observations* • *Witness observations* • *Artist observations* • *Employer* • *Observations* • *Family observations* • *Peer observations*
Worked towards their targets	• *Questionnaires* • *Activity Review Sheet* • *Evaluation Forms* • *Feedback sessions* • *Diary/Logbook* • *Timelines*	• *Certificates* • *Test results*	• *Witness observations* • *Peer observations* • *Attendance records*
Took the appropriate amount of responsibility	• *Role descriptions* • *Work plans* • *Task Sheets* • *Diary/Logbook* • *Activity Review Sheet*	• *Role descriptions* • *Work plans* • *Task Sheets* • *Diary/Logbook* • *Activity Review Sheet*	